Other *Chicken Soup for the Soul*® Titles
Available in Trade Paperback and Hardcover

Chicken Soup for the Mother's Soul 2

Chicken Soup for the Parent's Soul

Chicken Soup for the Pet Lover's Soul

Chicken Soup for the Preteen Soul

Chicken Soup for the Single's Soul

Chicken Soup for the Sports Fan's Soul

Chicken Soup for the Surviving Soul

Chicken Soup for the Teenage Soul

Chicken Soup for the Teenage Soul II

Chicken Soup for the Teenage Soul III

Chicken Soup for the Teenage Soul Journal

Chicken Soup for the Teenage Soul Letters

Chicken Soup for the Unsinkable Soul

Chicken Soup for the Woman's Soul

A Second Chicken Soup for the Woman's Soul

Chicken Soup for the Writer's Soul

Chicken Soup for the Soul® at Work

Chicken Soup for the Soul® Cookbook

Sopa de pollo para el alma *(Spanish language version)*

All *Chicken Soup for the Soul* titles are also
available on audiotape and CD.

A CUP OF CHICKEN SOUP FOR THE SOUL®

Stories to Open the Heart and Rekindle the Spirit

Jack Canfield
Mark Victor Hansen
Barry Spilchuk

Health Communications, Inc.
Deerfield Beach, Florida

www.bci-online.com
www.chickensoup.com

Library of Congress Cataloging-in-Publication Data

A cup of chicken soup for the soul: stories to open the
  heart and rekindle the spirit / [compiled by] Jack Canfield,
  Mark Victor Hansen, and Barry Spilchuk.
      p.   cm.
    ISBN 1-55874-421-5 (trade paper)
    ISBN 1-55874-947-0 (mass-market paperback)
    1. Conduct of life.   2. Spiritual life.   3. Inspiration—
Anecdotes.   I. Canfield, Jack, date.   II. Hansen, Mark Victor.
III. Spilchuk, Barry, date.
BJ1581.2C87 1996
158'.12—dc20   96-32299
                                                          CIP

First mass-market paperback edition published by Health
Communications, Inc., 2001.

Publisher: Health Communications, Inc.
                3201 S.W. 15th Street
                Deerfield Beach, FL 33442-8190

R-09-01

Cover redesign and typesetting by Lawna Patterson Oldfield

*Thinking: The talking of
the soul with itself.*

Plato

The stories in this book were chosen to make you think: think about yourself, think about your family, think about your friends and think about love; for it is with love that all great things are accomplished.

It is with love and heartfelt gratification that we dedicate this book to our wives, Georgia, Patty and Karen, and to our children Christopher, Oran, Kyle, Elisabeth, Melanie, Jamie, Christine and Michael. Your wisdom, caring, love and support have allowed us to express ourselves fully and soulfully.

Contents

2. ON PARENTS & CHILDREN

3. OVERCOMING OBSTACLES

4. ON REMEMBERING

5. ON ATTITUDE

6. EVERYDAY HEROES

7. ECLECTIC WISDOM

Acknowledgments

This book is the first mini-offspring of the successful *Chicken Soup for the Soul* series. It has taken the love and labor of many for the better part of a year to deliver this book to you. We would like to thank the following people for their contributions, without which this book would still be just an idea:

Peter Vegso and Gary Seidler at Health Communications, for continuing to share our vision and giving us their full support and encouragement.

Our wives and our children who constantly support us with their love, emotional support, story editing, evaluating and never-ending belief in us and the dream we all share of touching people's souls and teaching them how to love.

Patty Aubery, who was the main flag-waver for this project from the start. Patty, we love you! Her constant challenge to us was to make this a great book. We feel we have met her challenge.

Nancy Mitchell, who has become a one-person resource-bank of valuable insight into what our readers want and what our legal department needs in order to satisfy the hundreds of permissions necessary to give this book its integrity and focus. Thank you, Nancy. We love you.

Heather McNamara, who oversaw every aspect of the editing, writing, compiling and completion of this book. Her dedication to the project and her willingness to always go the extra mile made this book possible.

Kim Wiele, whose insistence that *all* the stories be from the heart, kept us focused and on track.

Veronica Valenzuela, Julie Knapp, Ro Miller and Anna Maria Flores for doing all the things necessary to help us stay on track. We appreciate all of their efforts.

Lisa Williams, for keeping Mark balanced and on track.

Mary Jo Racine for the countless hours spent researching and typing new stories.

Aimee Kunkel, for her "whatever-it-takes"

attitude to help us bring this project to a conclusion in record time.

Trudy Klefstad at OfficeWorks for her computer support and Internet expertise.

Christine Belleris, Matthew Diener and Mark Colucci, our editors at Health Communications—working with these friendly professionals has been a wonderful and pleasing experience.

Our love to Karen Spilchuk for reading *every* story and giving it her loving and honest opinion.

Jamie, Crissy and Mike Spilchuk for helping get the book ready for its final stages by numbering pages and searching for author histories. We love you.

Paul Barton, Barry's number one mastermind partner, who kept challenging him to go for it and do whatever it took to bring this project to fruition on time.

Sharon Ro, Brenda Rose, Marci Shimoff, Robyn Kalama, Sandy Rifkin and Mary Peterson, who kept us in alignment with our vision.

Ann Taylor, Dennis Smith and Don Hull of Crawford & Company—their belief in our vision has been a blessing.

Bernie and Lynn Dohrmann and the

7,000 graduates of the Income Builders International Free Enterprise Forum. This is where we met as a team to envision and create this new work of love for our readers.

Valerie Gill, for her unconditional love and support of us and our project. She phoned all over North America to ensure we had new and loving stories to give to our audience.

Scott Clark, Master DJ at MIX 100.5, Dave McLellan and John Tollesfrud of the *North Bay Nugget*, Linda Holmes of MCTV and Wolf Hess of CBC Radio for the amazing amount of media exposure they gave us to kickoff this project.

Bev Broughton and Peggy Walsh Craig for being the first to send in stories for this book. Their enthusiasm for this project allowed us to begin with a running start.

The people of North Bay and Northern Ontario for overwhelmingly getting behind this project with their stories and encouragement to make it the first *Chicken Soup* book to be started in Canada.

Nipissing University, Canadore College and the North Bay Public Library for opening their research files and libraries to enable us to "surf the Net" and scan the history books.

Tom and Becky Stambaugh, the real life Mr. and Mrs. Santa Claus, who sent us more stories than anyone else. When we are with them it always seems like Christmas.

Joyce Spilchuk and Dorothy Belanger for being named cowinners of the Queen of the Quotations award. Both of these precious people sent in dozens and dozens of quotations for us to peruse. Many of their finds are published here.

Paula Petrovic, who gave us the tools to love and nurture this new creation from inception to completion.

Eugene and Tim Spilchuk, for believing in Barry's vision and dream.

The more than 5,000 people who submitted stories, poems and anecdotes for consideration—you know who you are. We gratefully acknowledge your efforts and your submissions. While we wish we could publish them all, many of them did not fit the overall structure of this book. Many of your stories may be used in future volumes.

We also want to thank the following people who read the rough draft of 160 stories, helped us make the final selections and made very helpful comments on how to improve the book: Paul Barton (Barry's coauthor of *The Magic of Masterminding*), Jill Bentley, Patricia Carr, Tom Chavez, Paulette Chang, Scott Clark, Carol Conrad, Maureen Corral, Janina Daly, Marilyn Duvall, Christy and Ann Ellis, Yves Gervais, Nancy Richard-Guilford, James Guilford, Janet Hagerman, Adoria Kante, Donna Loesch, Jill Miller, Cheryl Myers, Dana Ouderkerk, Joyce Spilchuk, Kathy Spilchuk, and Mary Jane West-Delgado.

Arielle Ford and Kim Weiss, our publicists who keep us busy on radio, television and in the papers so we can spread the word.

Because this project was such a huge undertaking we have probably left out a few names of some very important people who helped us along the way—everyone from Barry's neighbors who helped with the family while Barry moved to Santa Barbara for *two* months to finish the project to all the people who have helped in any way. We apologize for the oversight and sincerely appreciate all of you from the bottom of our hearts for all your love and attention to this project.

Finally, to the millions people who now own at least one member of the *Chicken Soup for the Soul* family of books, we thank you for your faith in our vision and ongoing support of our projects. It is with love that we have created this book for *you!*

Introduction

From our hearts to yours, we are delighted to offer you *A Cup of Chicken Soup for the Soul*. This book contains stories, cartoons and quotations that will uplift and inspire you to love more unconditionally, live more passionately, and pursue your heart's desire with more conviction and confidence. This book will sustain you in times of challenge, frustration and failure, and comfort you in times of confusion, pain and loss. It will truly become a lifelong companion, offering continual insight and wisdom in many areas of your life.

We believe that you are about to embark on a truly remarkable experience. Our first books, *Chicken Soup for the Soul, A 2nd Helping of Chicken Soup for the Soul, A 3rd Serving of Chicken Soup for the Soul, The Chicken Soup for the Soul Cookbook* and *Chicken Soup for the Surviving Soul (101 Stories of Courage and*

Inspiration from Those Who Have Survived Cancer) have deeply touched the lives of more than 8 million readers around the world.

We appreciatively receive hundreds of letters a week that tell of the miracles of transformation that occur as a result of reading the books and following their advice. Our readers report that the love, hope, encouragement and inspiration they have found in these stories has profoundly impacted their lives.

You may be tempted to read this book in one sitting—many people have done that with good results. We, however, recommend that you slow down and take the time to savor and digest each story. This will allow you to enjoy *A Cup of Chicken Soup for the Soul* one "sip" at a time.

Share with Us

Many people have inspired us with their stories over the years, and we are grateful to them. We hope that in some way we will be part of inspiring you to love and live more fully. If we achieve that, we have been successful.

Finally, we would love to hear your reactions to this book. Please write to us and tell us how these stories affect you. Also, we invite you to become part of this wonderful "network of upliftment" by sending us your stories.

Stories are like fairy gold. The more you give away the more you have.

Polly McGuire

Please send us any stories, poems and cartoons you think we should include in future volumes of *Chicken Soup for the Soul.*

See page 217 for our address. We look forward to hearing from you. Until then, may you enjoy reading *A Cup of Chicken Soup for the Soul* as much as we have enjoyed compiling, editing and writing it.

Jack Canfield, Mark Victor Hansen
and Barry Spilchuk

$\overline{1}$

ON LOVE

A bell's not a bell
'til you ring it
A song's not a song
'til you sing it
Love in your heart
wasn't put there to stay
Love isn't love
'til you give it away!

Oscar Hammerstein

Important Work

The last to board the plane from Seattle to Dallas were a woman and three children. "Oh, please, don't sit next to me," I thought. "I've got so much work to do." But a moment later an eleven-year-old girl and her nine-year-old brother were climbing over me while the woman and a four-year-old boy sat behind. Almost immediately the older children started bickering while the child behind intermittently kicked my seat. Every few minutes the boy would ask his sister, "Where are we now?" "Shut up!" she'd snap and a new round of squirming and whining would ensue.

"Kids have no concept of important work," I thought, quietly resenting my predicament. Then in my mind a voice as clear as a song simply said, *Love them.* "These kids are brats, and I've got important work to do," I countered to myself. My inner voice simply replied, *Love them as if they were your children.*

Having heard the "Where-are-we-now?" question repeatedly, I turned to the in-flight magazine map in spite of my important work.

I explained our flight path, dividing it into quarter-hour flight increments and estimated when we would land in Dallas.

Soon they were telling me about their trip to Seattle to see their father who was in the hospital. As we talked they asked about flying, navigation, science and grown-ups' views about life. The time passed quickly and my "important" work was left undone.

As we were preparing to land, I asked how their father was doing now. They grew quiet and the boy simply said, "He died."

"Oh, I'm so sorry."

"Yeah, me too. But it's my little brother I'm most worried about. He's taking it real hard."

I suddenly realized what we'd really been talking about was the most important work we ever face: living, loving and growing in spite of heartbreak. When we said good-bye in Dallas the boy shook my hand and thanked me for being his "airline teacher." And I thanked him for being mine.

Dan S. Bagley

An Angel Flew My Way

I have photographed children for more than twenty years. One Thanksgiving I received a special gift from one of them. Emily was sitting on the floor all dressed in white. She was a cuddly six-month-old reclining in her carrier.

"Emily's not doing well today," the mom said. The little girl did seem flushed and her head wobbled from side to side as she tried to sit up straight. I tried several exposures but to no avail. Finally, I got close to Emily's face and started talking to her. "You look like an angel," I said.

Suddenly the child paused and her wobbly head came to attention. She looked at me as if to say, "I'm okay, I just had a bad day." Since Emily looks like an angel, that's the way I'm going to photograph her! I decided.

In my studio I keep a set of pure white angel wings made out of real duck down, soft and white. I also gave her a small crown of flowers. Cuddled in her seat and nestled in the clouds I began to photograph my angel.

I hadn't noticed, but the mother was softly crying. "She is an angel. We just found out yesterday that she was born with a rare brain defect. This will be our first and last Thanksgiving together," she sobbed. "They don't live past the first year. When I was carrying her, I did everything the doctor said to do. No smoking, I watched my diet, but her brain will not develop any more than it did at birth. There are only 435 known cases of this rare defect.

"You saw Emily here for what she really is, an angel, and we love her so. She's our little angel that fluttered down to earth to tell us that God wants us to appreciate what we have. You saw that in her, too. Sometimes you can be talking to her and she becomes so peaceful and calm. She starts to baby talk and you can almost make out her words. It's as if she's really trying to tell you something. These pictures are really important. We don't know how much longer she'll be with us. You've captured our little angel forever."

With a lump in my throat I said, "Thank you for sharing your little angel with me. I'm thankful she flew in my direction!"

Larry Miller

Missed Opportunities

I had offered to watch my three-year-old daughter, Ramanda, so that my wife could go out with a friend. I was getting some work done while Ramanda appeared to be having a good time in the other room. No problem, I figured. But then it got a little too quiet and I yelled out, "What are you doing, Ramanda?" No response. I repeated my question and heard her say, "Oh . . . nothing." *Nothing? What does "nothing" mean?*

I got up from my desk and ran out into the living room, whereupon I saw her take off down the hall. I chased her up the stairs and watched as her little behind made a hard left into the bedroom. I was gaining on her! She took off for the bathroom. Bad move. I had her cornered. I told her to turn around. She refused. I pulled out my big, mean, authoritative Daddy voice, "Young lady, I said turn around!"

Slowly, she turned toward me. In her hand was what was left of my wife's new lipstick. And every square inch of her face was covered with bright red (except her lips of course)!

As she looked up at me with fearful eyes, lips trembling, I heard every voice that had shouted to me as a child, "How could you? . . . You should know better than that . . . How many times have you been told? . . . What a bad thing to do. . . ." It was just a matter of my picking out which old message I was going to use on her so that she would know what a bad girl she had been. But before I could let loose, I looked down at the sweatshirt my wife had put on her only an hour before. In big letters it said, "I'M A PERFECT LITTLE ANGEL!" I looked back up into her tearful eyes and, instead of seeing a bad girl who didn't listen, I saw a child of God . . . a perfect little angel full of worth, value and a wonderful spontaneity that I had come dangerously close to shaming out of her.

"Sweetheart, you look beautiful! Let's take a picture so Mommy can see how special you look." I took the picture and thanked God that I didn't miss the opportunity to reaffirm what a perfect little angel he had given me.

Nick Lazaris

THE BUCKETS reprinted by permission of United Feature Syndicate, Inc.

Brian

Brian is seven. He's a dreamer and drives his teacher crazy. She's stiff as taffy in December.

One day Brian got to school an hour late. His teacher stormed from the classroom, down to the office, and called Brian's mother. "Brian was an hour late today," his teacher said. "I've just about had it!"

Brian's mother worried all day. Finally, Brian got home.

"Brian, what happened at school?"

"I was late. My teacher got mad."

"I know, Brian. She called me. What happened?"

"Well," Brian started, "it must have rained. There were worms all over the sidewalk." He paused a while and went on. "I knew the kids would step on them, so I tried to put them back in the holes."

He looked up at his mother. "It took a long time because they didn't want to go."

His mother hugged him. "I love you, Brian," she said.

Jay O'Callahan

We can only learn to love by loving.

Iris Murdoch

The Blue Rose

For years I became romantically involved with men who weren't emotionally available or capable of making a long-term commitment. My relationships were full of pain. I wanted to get married so I knew I had to do something radically different.

One day I decided to pray. "God, I don't know how to pick the right partner, so please, *please* choose my Divine Beloved for me, and prepare us both for our upcoming union. And God, just so I'm sure to know who you've chosen for me, let him somehow present me with a *blue rose.*"

Every day after that for five months I affirmed that my Divine Beloved was coming to me and that we would recognize each other at the right time.

Every day I let go of a little more control and opened a little more to God loving me.

And every day I looked for my blue rose.

Twelve days after I left my abusive boyfriend, I attended a networking luncheon where Alan Cohen was speaking. He spoke about the power each of us has to bless another human being. It touched me so deeply that when he invited us all to do a blessing exercise I was the first to jump out of my chair. More than 100 people around me scrambled to find a partner.

Suddenly everything was quiet and a young blue-eyed man stood in front of me. We joined hands and gazed into each other's eyes. Following the exercise I asked, "Will you bless me?" For several minutes he silently poured unconditional love and blessings onto me. He then asked, "Will you bless me?" and I returned the love. We didn't say anything else to each other.

The exercise ended and we returned to our seats. I was in a daze. In a few minutes the young man returned and introduced himself as David Rose. I knew then that God himself had presented me with my *blue-eyed Rose.*

A year later we married.

Brenda Rose

*To love and be loved
is to feel the sun
from both sides.*

David Viscott

Foreign Exchange

We met and greeted Andrea as she got off the chartered bus with the rest of the students from her country. These were foreign exchange students from Slovakia. Andrea spoke English, but she was very nervous. I could understand her trepidation; we were a family of five. The kids were so used to having foreign students around that they just walked right up to her and wanted to hug her, but as we found out later, she was unfamiliar with the hugging part. We hug a lot! We hug each other many times each day, and Andrea was watching it all. I could see the expression on her face each time she saw us hugging. She loved it. She wanted it.

She told me of her youth in Europe. Basically her mother was very loving and they had a loving relationship, as Andrea said, "in a European sort of way." She had not been held by her mother since she was a small child.

While living with us for the summer of 1992, Andrea became part of our family. We grew to love each other very quickly, and we hugged.

She learned the joys of hugging, and most of all she learned that she needed to share this emotional experience with her mother.

At the end of August, Andrea returned to Slovakia. She flew to Munich, where her mother met her at the airport. Her mother was in for the surprise of her life. Andrea's mother greeted her with her usual loving smile and words, and she helped Andrea carry her bags.

Andrea lovingly took her mother by the arm and said, "Mummy, I want to give you a hug." Andrea related that for only a moment her mother didn't know what to do. Andrea looked into her mother's eyes, tears in both of their eyes, and she said, "Mummy, I need to hug you, and I need for you to hug me, *a lot!*" They did just that. They didn't move an inch from the arrival area of the airport. Andrea said that they sat there for the next three hours. They cried.

They hugged. They talked. They cried more, hugged more and talked forever. Andrea says she will raise her own children with a lot of hugging. She says that her mother wants to be a big part of that, too.

Mary Jane West-Delgado

Universal Rx

No moving parts, no batteries,
No monthly payments and no fees;
Inflation proof, nontaxable,
In fact, it's quite relaxable.

It can't be stolen, won't pollute,
One size fits all, do not dilute.
It uses little energy,
But yields results enormously.

Relieves your tension and your stress,
Invigorates your happiness;
Combats depression, makes you beam,
And elevates your self-esteem!

Your circulation it corrects
Without unpleasant side effects.
It is, I think, the perfect drug:
May I prescribe, my friends . . . the hug!

(And, of course, fully returnable!)

Henry Matthew Ward

Simply Said

Fresh flowers are such a lovely thing of beauty. Once in a while I pick a bouquet or a single perfect rose to give to a neighbor, friend or relative.

Early one morning I gathered a beautiful bouquet of sweet-smelling, long-stemmed roses for myself. The roses were definitely a delight for my eyes. While I thought about how pleasing they were for me to enjoy, a calm, gentle voice outside of myself simply said, *Give them to your friend.*

I went straight into the house and arranged the roses in a vase. Then I wrote this note as small as I could . . . *For my friend.* I went across the street to my neighbor's, who is also one of my closest friends, and I left the bouquet at the front door.

Later that day my friend called to thank me. She said the flowers were a true blessing.

Late the night before she had been arguing with one of her children. Being cruel, as teenagers can sometimes be, her child said to her, "You have no friends."

What a surprise when she went to leave for work that morning and found not just the blessing of the bouquet of flowers, but also the tiny note which simply said, *"For my friend."*

Roberta Tremblay

The supreme happiness in life is the conviction that we are loved.

Victor Hugo

Beattitudes

Blessed are they who understand
My faltering step and crippled hand.
Blessed are they that know my ears today
Must strain to hear the things they say.

Blessed are they that seem to know
That my eyes are dim and my answers slow.
Blessed are they who look away
When my tea was spilled at the table today.

Blessed are they with a cheery smile
Who stopped to chat for a little while.
Blessed are they that never say
You have told that story twice today.

Blessed are they that make it known
That I am loved and not alone.
Blessed is my doctor who is the best you see
When I can't go to him then he will come to
    me.

Blessed are all that ease the days
Of my sunset years in loving ways.
Blessed are my family who are so very dear
Their good care is why I am still here.

Grace McDonald

I "Heard" the Love

When I was growing up I do not recall hearing the words "I love you" from my father. When your father never says them to you when you are a child, it gets tougher and tougher for him to say those words as he gets older. To tell the truth, I could not honestly remember when I had last said those words to him either. I decided to set my ego aside and make the first move. After some hesitation, in our next phone conversation I blurted out the words, "Dad . . . I love you!"

There was a silence at the other end and he awkwardly replied, "Well, same back at ya!"

I chuckled and said, "Dad, I know you love me, and when you are ready, I know you will say what you want to say."

Fifteen minutes later my mother called

and nervously asked, "Paul, is everything okay?"

A few weeks later, Dad concluded our phone conversation with the words, "Paul, I love you." I was at work during this conversation and the tears were rolling down my cheeks as I finally "heard" the love. As we both sat there in tears we realized that this special moment had taken our father/son relationship to a new level.

A short while after this special moment, my father narrowly escaped death following heart surgery. Many times since, I have pondered the thought, *If I did not take the first step and Dad did not survive the surgery, I would have never "heard" the love.*

Paul Barton

*N*ever part without loving words to think of during your absence. It may be that you will not meet again in life.

Jean Paul Richter

To Our Baby Girl

We both love you, and
We both have hopes and dreams for your
   future.

She carried you in her body for nine
   months;
I carried you in my dreams for five years.

She labored through birth;
I labored through INS, social workers and
   foreign law.

She is nature;
I am nurture.

She wonders if are you healthy;
I sit and rock you wondering when your
   fever will go down.

She wonders if you have enough to eat;
I wonder should I make you eat your
    broccoli.

She wonders if are you happy;
I love to hear you laugh.

She wonders if are you loved;
My heart melts with every smile and
    breaks with every tear I soothe.

She wonders what you look like;
I proudly display your pictures all over the
    house.

She hopes you get a good education;
I sit and help you with your homework
    every night.

She wonders what you will grow up to be
    like;
I teach you to be strong, independent and
    to believe in yourself.

She wonders if you will marry and have
    children;
I help you plan your wedding day and cry
    when I hold my grandchild for the first
    time.

She gave you life;
I am grateful to her every day that you are
    a part of my life.

She will always wonder about you;
I will always be thankful to her for
    bringing you into this world.

She will always be your biological mother;
I will always be Mommy.

Audrie LaVigne

"He's playing with me now.
You can't have him."

*You get to know
yourself when your son
says to you, "You know,
Dad, you put a higher
priority on your career
than you did on helping
us grow up."*

George Ignatieff

One Moment Please

"So, how do you develop a relationship?"
This question was asked of me when I was
doing a Relationship Service seminar for the
YMCA. I have to admit that the question
caught me off guard for a brief second. We
had been talking "theory" all day and this
woman wanted some concrete methods for
developing client or, for that matter, any
relationships.

After pausing for a minute to collect my
thoughts, I stated that the only thing I
could do was tell her the truth from my
experience. Somewhat shyly, I began to tell
her the story of how my wife and I saved
our relationship. My mind flashed back to a
time when Karen and I were at a State Fair
and I won two red velvet hearts as a conso-
lation prize in one of the midway games. I
broke apart the two hearts and gave one to

Karen and kept one for myself.

We had been married for ten years and we were going through a bit of a "flat spot" in our relationship. We still loved each other, but something was missing.

Karen did not want the "flatness" to continue so one day she came up with a plan. She took one of the hearts and hid it in my towel while I was taking a shower. When I went to grab my towel, the red heart spilled out. As I bent down to pick it up, I was overcome with a rush of emotion that made me flash back to the time when I won the red hearts and the love we felt for each other at that moment.

I then hid the heart in her sock drawer. She hid it in my underwear drawer. I hid it in the refrigerator. She wrapped it in plastic wrap and hid it in the peanut butter. Hiding the heart became as much fun as finding it. Each time we hid or found it was a moment to be treasured, like the first moment we fell in love or the first moment we kissed or the first moment we looked into our child's eyes. Each is a cherished and precious moment.

How do you develop a relationship? One *moment* at a time!

Barry Spilchuk

Life isn't a matter
of milestones
But of moments.

Rose Kennedy

2

ON PARENTS & CHILDREN

If you want your children to turn out well, spend twice as much time with them and half as much money on them.

Abigail Van Buren

Making Jeffrey's "Best Day!"

When three of my grandchildren acquired a half-grown mongrel I agreed to help them build a doghouse.

As we began the project, I knew that keeping them involved was going to be a challenge. Much of my energy was spent calling them back to the job and finding parts of the project that could be handled by small children. I held to my initial determination that building this doghouse was to be a group project.

Early in the project I had promised the grandkids that we would roast wieners in the backyard as soon as we finished painting the canine residence. Selecting three of the largest house-painting brushes I could find, I supervised the painting of our homemade structure. Kids and paint. How could I have forgotten the potential mayhem that such a combination can create?

After cleaning up the paint mess—kids, brushes, carport—I suggested that we would probably eat earlier if we just asked Gramma to heat the wieners in water on the gas range. A pain of guilt came over me as I realized I was trying to weasel out of an earlier promise.

As Jamie, Jeffrey and Kimberley looked on, I built a first-class fire in our backyard pit, whittled some roasting sticks and prepared for the outdoor cooking event.

When we finished eating I leaned back on the cool grass and watched the last flickering remnants of our fire. Six-year-old Jeffrey was leaning back against my chest, and I began to think about what it meant to be a Grampa. The silence was broken when Jeffrey quietly reflected, "Know what Grampa?" And without breaking his gaze at the dying embers he continued, "This is the best day of my whole life."

After a few moments of continued silence he glanced up and said, "Are you crying, Grampa? You've got a tear on your cheek." Clearing my throat, I explained that it must be from the smoke.

Frank Cooper

From the Heart of
a Joyous Child

Dear Mommy and Daddy,

I write this letter to you in hopes that you will consider your approach to parenting me before I arrive. I am a joyous child. I thrive on love and respect, order and consistency. When I arrive, I will seem very small to you. Even though I don't look like an adult, please understand that I am a human being.

Even though I will not speak words to you, I will know you with my heart. I will feel all your feelings, absorb your thoughts. I will come to know you more than you may know yourself. Do not be misled by my silence. I am open, growing and learning more rapidly than you can imagine.

I will make imprints of all that I see, so please give me beauty to rest my eyes upon.

I will record all that I hear, so please give me sweet music and language that tells me how much I am loved. Give me silence to rest my ears. I will absorb all that I feel, so please wrap our life in love.

I am waiting patiently to be with you. I am so happy to have the opportunity to be alive. Maybe when you see me you will remember how precious life is too!

Your joyous child

Donna McDermott

*To understand your parents' love,
you must raise children yourself.*
Chinese proverb

A Christmas Toast

After putting up our Christmas tree on a Sunday evening, I told my two sons that it was time to get ready for bed. Justin said he thought it would be nice to sit as a family and admire the tree together. He asked if we could all do that for a minute before bed.

Although it was late, I decided to let him have the minute he wanted. I told him it was a great idea and I suggested we have a drink of eggnog by the tree and have a "toast" to welcome the Christmas season. He was so excited, he ran to the kitchen and got the eggnog from the fridge. I got my best crystal liquor glasses and he filled them up. I took the glasses to the coffee table by the tree and called for my older son who had left the room.

Once we were seated by the tree with our eggnog, I again called for Justin. For some reason he had not come back into the living room after pouring the eggnog.

Justin answered by saying, "I'm coming, Mom, it'll just be a minute, the toast is almost done!"

He was in the kitchen making toast! My husband and I could barely contain our laughter as Justin emerged from the kitchen with a plate on which he had a slice of toast, torn into four pieces, and exclaimed, "Okay, we're ready now, I've got the Christmas Toast!"

We sat by the tree, drinking our eggnog and eating a piece of dry toast while admiring the tree. We still haven't told him what "to make a toast" means as he was so proud of himself for what he had done. The look on his face that evening still brings tears to my eyes. He was so happy and I was so happy that I didn't insist on them going to bed right away like I normally would have. I learned that sometimes when you give a minute, you can gain a lot more.

Kelly Ranger

The Bigger the Better

Karen and I were the proud "Parents of the Day" at our son, Michael's, kindergarten class. We had fun as he toured us around his classroom and introduced us to all his friends. We joined in for cut and paste and sewing and spent the better part of the morning in the sandbox. It was a riot!

"Circle up!" called the teacher. "It's story time." Not wanting to look out of place, Karen and I "circled up" with the rest of our new buddies. After finishing the story, entitled *Big,* the teacher asked this enthusiastic group, "What makes you feel big?"

"Bugs make me feel big," yelled one young student. "Ants," hollered another. "Mosquitoes," called out one more.

The teacher, trying to bring some order back to the class, started calling on children with their hands up. Pointing to one little girl, the teacher said, "Yes, dear, what makes you feel big?" "My mommy," was the reply.

"How does your mommy make you feel big?" quizzed the teacher. "That's easy," said the child. "When she hugs me and says 'I love you, Jessica!'"

Barry Spilchuk

"This is my favorite place—
inside your hug."

More Gas

Bob's father was a car salesman in Stockton. His car was his pride and joy—a 1958 Cadillac. You know, one of those "boats" about a block long with fins that reached practically to heaven and carefully cared for, as only a man's car can be cared for. It was never left out in the weather and was faithfully washed and waxed. It was a shining example of a man's treasured wheels. Bob had just turned sixteen and had his driver's license. His father, seeing his burning desire to get behind the wheel of that Cadillac, gave him three dollars and sent him to get gasoline.

Bursting with pride and filled with youthful enthusiasm, Bob drove to the station, and sat with a big smile on his face as the station attendant filled the tank, washed the windows and checked the oil and tire pressure (remember this was 1960!).

Then, the unthinkable happened. As he pulled away, Bob cut the corner too sharply and scraped the whole side of the car along a brick pillar. He felt a sickening thud in his stomach and, for a moment, he considered running away. The thought of facing his father was awful. He didn't know which would be worse, his father's anger or his disappointment. Either way, he knew he had to go back and face him. He drove home, parked the car, and with his heart in his throat and his head bowed, a somber sixteen-year-old went in to get his father.

They came back out together to survey the damage—and it was considerable. Bob says they stood there for what seemed like an eternity, his father saying nothing. Finally, Bob looked at him and in a trembling voice said, "Dad, what do you want me to do?"

Deliberately his father reached into his back pocket for his wallet and took out two dollars. Handing it to Bob and looking him straight in the eye, he said, "Son, I think you better go back and get some more gas."

Cari Morrison

He's Not
My Stepfather!

My mother died when I was eight years old. It was very sad for everyone. Six months later, my father met Cathy. She had two kids, Megan and Griffin. I loved them from the very first time I saw them. I didn't realize how much, though.

A year and a half later, my father married Cathy. They were very much in love. At the wedding, I realized how much I loved Megan and Griffin. From then on, until we found a new house big enough for our new family, we kept switching back and forth between our house and Cathy's house as we were merging our two families. One night we were at Cathy's and we were lining up to give Cathy kisses. Griffin was last in line. After he kissed Cathy, she said, "Grif, give your stepfather a kiss."

And Griffin very angrily said, "He's not my stepfather! He's my dad!"

Jayne Kelley

The most lasting honors
of all are those which
your own family
bestows on you.

O. A. Battista

Two for the Price of One

"Where's Jamie?" screamed my cousin Lee Ann. "Oh my God, where *is* Jamie?" I thought, as we were standing in the pool at my parents' house. The question about my five-year-old son's momentary disappearance sent shock waves through my body.

The entire pool has a safety ledge around the inside of it and gently slopes to a deep end of only four feet. It was very common for us to let the younger children splash their afternoons away in Grandma's pool while we stood beside them and got totally soaked with their enthusiasm and the water.

On that scary afternoon when Lee Ann yelled, it seems that Jamie had been walking near the safety ledge and slid down into the deeper part. We had taken our eyes off him for only a split second, and then he was gone! I quickly spotted him and reached down to pull him up.

As I yanked him up, he came out kicking and screaming, crying and fearful, and yelling that he wanted to get out. My guilt wanted to take him out and grant him his wish, but my fatherly instincts told me to stay in the pool with him. Both of us were shaking as I talked to him and reassured him that water can be scary and we must respect it. I held him close as we gently walked around the pool. After a couple of minutes he said he wasn't afraid anymore and he started to splash around again.

I was feeling guilty and sorry for myself for being such a bad father. "Good fathers don't let their sons almost drown," I was telling myself. Just at the height of my personal pity party, Lee Ann walked by and said, "You are a terrific dad and I really admire the way you handled that. He will never be afraid of the water again!"

Lee Ann saved two lives that day. She saved my son's life when she yelled "Where's Jamie?" and she saved my life as a father! She took me from pity to pride with her nurturing comment. It's amazing what can happen when you look at yourself through someone else's eyes.

Barry Spilchuk

In the Eye of the Beholder

One night, my eight-year-old son, Zakariya, and I were scanning the TV listings for something to watch.

"Oooh, there's a beauty contest on," I said. Zakariya asked me what a beauty contest was, and I explained that it was a contest to choose the most beautiful woman in the world.

Then my son thrilled me by asking, with complete sincerity, "Why aren't you in the contest, Mommy?"

Tammy Litchfield Najjar
Excerpted from Woman's World

"Why do you hafta use Oil of Old Lady?"

A Tribute to Mother

Your hands once busy through the day,
You didn't have much time to play.
The little games I asked you, too,
You never had much time to do.
I 'd bring my color book to share my fun.
You'd say, "A little later, Hon."
You tucked me in all safe at night,
Hear my prayers, turn out the light,
Then tiptoe softly to the door.
I wish you'd stayed a moment more.
For life is short, the years rush past.
A little child grows up so fast.
No longer are you at my side,
My precious secrets to confide.
The color books are put away.
There are no longer games to play.
No goodnight kiss, no prayers to hear.
That all belongs to yesteryear.

Your hands once busy, now lie still.
The days are long and hard to fill.
I wish we could go back and do
The little things I asked you to.
But that's okay, 'cause I love you still.
I always did and I always will.

MaryAnn LoSchiavo Barbuto

"Anytime you're ready, Daddy,
I'll be sitting outside growing older."

*The country clubs,
the cars, the boats,
Your assets may be ample,
But the best inheritance
You can leave your kids
Is to be a good example.*

Barry Spilchuk

Unconscious Freedom

Billy and Kay could hardly believe what they had just heard. *Mom and Dad were going to let them explore the amusement park all morning by themselves?* It was almost too good to be true. Why, that meant they could move through the park as fast as they wanted . . . from ride to ride to ride. It meant they could ride whatever rides they wanted—in whatever order—and as many times as they like. What freedom!

The only stipulations were that they were to stay together and were to meet at the central plaza at twelve noon sharp! Billy and Kay synchronized their watches with Dad, and off they went. What a morning they had! They even arrived at the plaza a few minutes before noon, glad for a little rest. "Do you think we should tell Mom about that creepy guy that followed us for awhile?" Billy asked.

"No," said Kay, "let's not worry her."

"Do you think I should admit to Dad that I left one of the souvenirs I bought on that next to the last ride?" Kay asked. "Naw," said Billy. "I wouldn't." "I can't believe they let us have all morning to explore on our own," Billy sighed. "Yeah," said Kay. "I guess they must think we're pretty grown up."

About that time, Mom and Dad showed up. "Did you guys have fun?" Mom asked. "Lots!" Kay said. "You'll never believe it," Dad said, holding up a little sack. "Your mom and I went on this one ride and somebody had left this behind in the car. It's pretty cool." "That was mine!" Kay shrieked. "I left it there. I can't believe you found it!"

"Did you see a creepy looking guy over in that one area of the park?" Mom asked. Billy said, "Yeah, we saw him. He was weird, but we ignored him."

It wasn't until ten years later that Billy and Kay found out Mom and Dad had been there all the time—just a few yards away, out of sight, having the time of their lives as they watched their children having the time of *their* lives!

This Little Light of Mine

"They look so sweet and peaceful when they're asleep. You wonder how they could ever yell at us during the day."

Family Circus Cartoons. *Reprinted with special permission of King Features Syndicate.*

*There are only
two lasting bequests
we can hope to give our
children: One of these is roots,
the other wings.*

Hodding Carter

Prime Time

Alex was heading out of town on an assignment for the newspaper he worked for. Actually, he was looking forward to being away from the office and from his hectic family schedule.

The family farewell had not gone very well before he left. Alex's wife, Deanne, was worrying about handling all the family responsibilities while he was away, and Alex was too busy to notice her distress.

In the midst of all the chaos, eight-year-old Matthew asked his father if he would be back to hear his class concert on Thursday evening. Alex replied, "Sorry, I'll be out of town."

He said good-bye quickly and walked out the door. The out-of-town assignment would take Alex and the newspaper photographer to the Columbia Gorge on the

Columbia River. As they approached the canyon, Alex noticed all the windsurfers and the sailboarders. It looked like the ideal life. Carefree. Worry-free. Responsibility-free. Alex wondered where he had gone wrong—how had he missed this good life?

As he sat in his motel room the last night of the assignment, Alex had a sense of emptiness, of not belonging. Not at home, not here, not anywhere. Things that had seemed important to him—God, marriage, children, work—were now slipping away from him.

Then, Alex noticed in his suitcase a greet-ing card tucked beneath some clothes. The card was from Deanne. It said, "I'll love you 'til the cows come home." He looked at the card and Deanne's familiar handwriting and melted inside. In that instant, Alex knew exactly where he belonged.

The next day, after a long news-feature interview and a rushed trip home, Alex raced to Matthew's concert, arriving just in time. As he rushed into the school audito-rium to sit down, Deanne jumped up to greet him in elated surprise, then led him to their seats. She had reserved two in the second row, "just in case." When Matthew saw them together as the band marched on stage, he grinned from ear to ear and waved wildly to say hello. Alex acknowledged him, stood up and waved back. Then he turned to Deanne and said, "It sure is good to be home."

This Little Light of Mine

*I work too hard.
I miss my spouse.
My kids think I'm a jerk.
Psst! No one has
said on their deathbed
I should have spent more
time at work!*

Barry Spilchuk

3

OVERCOMING OBSTACLES

It's kind of fun to do the impossible!

Walt Disney

Blind Ambition

Charlie Boswell has always been one of my heroes. He has inspired me and thousands of others to rise above circumstances and live our true passion. Charlie was blinded during World War II while rescuing his friend from a tank that was under fire. He was a great athlete before his accident, and in a testimony to his talent and determination he decided to try a brand-new sport, a sport he never imagined playing even with his eyesight . . . *golf!*

Through determination and a deep love for the game he became the National Blind Golf Champion! He won that honor thirteen times. One of his heroes was the great golfer Ben Hogan, so it truly was an honor for Charlie to win the Ben Hogan Award in 1958.

Upon meeting Ben Hogan, Charlie was awestruck and stated that he had one wish and it was to have one round of golf with the great Ben Hogan.

Mr. Hogan agreed that playing a round together would be an honor for him as well, as he had heard about all of Charlie's accomplishments and truly admired his skills.

"Would you like to play for money, Mr. Hogan?" blurted out Charlie.

"I can't play you for money; it wouldn't be fair!" said Mr. Hogan.

"Aw, come on, Mr. Hogan, $1,000 per hole!"

"I can't. What would people think of me, taking advantage of you and your circumstance?" replied the sighted golfer.

"Chicken, Mr. Hogan?"

"Okay," blurted a frustrated Hogan, "but I am going to play my best!"

"I wouldn't expect anything else," said the confident Boswell.

"You're on, Mr. Boswell. You name the time and the place!"

A very self-assured Boswell responded "ten o'clock . . . *tonight!*"

John Kanary

Special Orders

Horror gripped the heart of the World War I soldier as he saw his lifelong friend fall in battle. Caught in a trench with continuous gunfire whizzing over his head, the soldier asked his lieutenant if he might go out into the "No Man's Land" between the trenches to bring his fallen comrade back.

"You can go," said the lieutenant, "but I don't think it will be worth it. Your friend is probably dead and you may throw your own life away." The lieutenant's words didn't matter, and the soldier went anyway.

Miraculously he managed to reach his friend, hoist him onto his shoulder and bring him back to their company's trench. As the two of them tumbled in together to the bottom of the trench, the officer checked the wounded soldier, then looked kindly at his friend. "I told you it wouldn't be worth it," he said. "Your friend is dead, and you are mortally wounded."

"It was worth it, though, sir," the soldier said.

"How do you mean, 'worth it'?" responded the lieutenant. "Your friend is dead!"

"Yes, sir," the private answered. "But it was worth it because when I got to him he was still alive, and I had the satisfaction of hearing him say, 'Jim, I knew you'd come.'"

This Little Light of Mine

A true friend is the greatest of all blessings and the one which we take the least thought to acquire.

François, Duc de La Rochefoucald

Out of a Jam

It was 1933. I had been laid off from my part-time job and could no longer make my contribution to the family larder. Our only income was what Mother could make by doing dressmaking for others. Then Mother was sick for a few weeks and unable to work. The electric company came out and cut off the power when we couldn't pay the bill. Then the gas company cut off the gas. Then the water company. But the Health Department made them turn the water back on for sanitation reasons. The cupboard got very bare. We had a vegetable garden and were able to cook some of its produce on a campfire in the backyard.

Then one day my younger sister came skipping home from school saying, "We're supposed to bring something to school tomorrow to give to the poor."

Mother started to blurt out, "I don't know of anyone who is any poorer than we are," when her mother, who was living with us at the time, shushed her with a hand on her arm and a frown.

"Eva," she said, "if you give that child the idea that she is 'poor folks' at her age, she will be 'poor folks' for the rest of her life. There is one jar of that homemade jelly left. She can take that."

Grandmother found some tissue paper and a little bit of pink ribbon with which she wrapped our last jar of jelly, and Sis tripped off to school the next day proudly carrying her "gift to the poor." After that, if there ever was a problem in the community, she just naturally assumed that she was supposed to be part of the solution.

Edgar Bledsoe

Persons thankful for little things are certain to be the ones with much to be thankful for.

Frank Clark

Nothing Could Stop This Man

After suffering severe burns on his legs at the age of five, Glenn Cunningham was given up on by doctors who believed he would be a hopeless cripple destined to spend the rest of his life in a wheelchair. "He will never be able to walk again," they said. "No chance."

The doctors examined his legs, but they had no way of looking into Glenn Cunningham's heart. He didn't listen to the doctors and set out to walk again. Lying in bed, his skinny, red legs covered with scar tissue, Glenn vowed, "Next week, I'm going to get out of bed. I'm going to walk." And he did just that.

His mother tells of how she used to push back the curtain and look out the window to watch Glenn reach up and take hold of an old plow in the yard. With a hand on each handle, he began to make his gnarled and twisted legs function. And with every step a step of pain, he came closer to walking. Soon he began to trot; before long he was running. When he started to run, he became even more determined.

"I always believed that I could walk, and I did. Now I'm going to run faster than anybody has ever run." And did he ever.

He became a great miler who, in 1934, set the world's record of 4:06. He was honored as the outstanding athlete of the century at Madison Square Garden.

Jeff Yalden

You may be disappointed if you fail, but you are doomed if you don't try.
Beverly Sills

Thelma

Even at the age of seventy-five, Thelma was very vivacious and full of life. When her husband passed away, her children suggested that she move to a "senior living community." A gregarious and life-loving person, Thelma decided to do so.

Shortly after moving in, Thelma became a self-appointed activities director, coordinating all sorts of things for the people in the community to do; she quickly became very popular and made many friends.

When Thelma turned eighty, her newfound friends showed their appreciation by throwing a surprise birthday party for her. When Thelma entered the dining room for dinner that night, she was greeted by a standing ovation and one of the coordinators led her to the head table. The night was filled with laughter and entertainment, but throughout the evening, Thelma could not take her eyes off a gentleman sitting at the other end of the table.

When the festivities ended, Thelma quickly rose from her seat and rushed over to the man. "Pardon me," Thelma said. "Please forgive me if I made you feel uncomfortable by staring at you all night. I just couldn't help myself from looking your way. You see, you look just like my fifth husband."

"Your fifth husband!" replied the gentleman. "Forgive me for asking, but how many times have you been married?"

With that, a smile came across Thelma's face as she responded, "Four."

They were married shortly after.

Shari Smith

Barriers

When I was little, Dibby's cousin had a dog, just a mutt, and the dog was pregnant. I don't know how long dogs remain pregnant, but she was due to have her puppies in about a week. She was out in the yard one day and got in the way of the lawn mower, and her two hind legs got cut off. They rushed her to the vet and he said, "I can sew her up, or you can put her to sleep if you want, but the puppies are okay. She'll be able to deliver the puppies."

Dibby's cousin said, "Keep her alive."

So the vet sewed up her backside and over the next week the dog learned to walk. She didn't spend any time worrying, she just learned to walk by taking two steps in the front and flipping up her backside, and then taking two steps and flipping up her backside again. She gave birth to six little puppies, all in perfect health. She nursed them and then weaned them. And when they learned to walk, they all walked like her.

Gilda Radner
From It's Always Something

*If I could wish for my
life to be perfect, it would be
tempting but I would
have to decline, for life
would no longer teach
me anything.*

Allyson Jones
From a Hallmark Shoebox
Greeting Card

The Qualities of Survival

Several years ago I found myself a long way from home in a small prison cell. As a prisoner of war, I was tortured, humiliated, starved and left to languish in squalor for six years.

It's important that you get a vivid mental picture of this scene. Try your best to smell the stench in the bucket I called my toilet and taste the salt in the corners of my mouth from my sweat, my tears and my blood. Feel the baking tropical heat in a tin roofed prison cell—not that you'll ever be a P.O.W. If I am effective in these few moments we spend together, you'll see that the same kind of challenges you face as a teenager, a student, a leader or a parent are the same basic challenges I faced in a prison cell: feelings of fear, loneliness, failure and a breakdown of communication.

More importantly, your response to those challenges will be the same response I had to have in the prison camp just to survive.

What qualities do you have within you that would allow you to survive in a prison camp? Please pause here, think about this question, and write in the margin of this page at least five different qualities necessary for survival. (If you've written faith, commitment or dedication, you've already broken the code.)

As I worked my way through the first several months and then years of imprisonment, I found I already had a foundation of survival tools learned in life from my parents, preachers, youth leaders and teachers. And the lifesaving techniques I used in that prison camp had more to do with my value system, integrity and religious faith than anything I had learned from a textbook.

Sound like your life? The adversities you face in your life can be just as debilitating to you as six years in a communist prison camp could have been to me. Now here's the test: The next time you have a huge problem facing you, turn back to this page and read not my writing but your writing in the margin. You'll find that the same factors you've written here, which would serve you well in a prison camp, will serve you even better in the challenge of everyday life.

Charlie Plumb

My Mascot

The nursing aides for the eighty-nine-year-old man planned a surprise party for him. This active and alert retired doctor had had his leg amputated two years ago. It had been a struggle to adjust to living his life with only one leg, spending most of his time in a wheelchair.

Family, friends and volunteers filled the brightly decorated room. He looked at the group and signaled a sweet six-year-old girl, the grandchild of one of his aides, to come over to him. He reached out and put his arm around her. He introduced her and announced, "She is my mascot!" He went on to tell the group assembled that he would never forget the first time she visited. She came in, looked at him and his folded up pants leg in the wheelchair, and in her charming voice asked, "Where is your prosthesis?" He was astounded she knew the word. She showed him her prosthesis and told him her story. When she was three years old, a man broke into her home, killed her seventeen-month-old brother and, with a machete, cut off her leg.

He said this young girl taught him not to complain and to be grateful for the eighty-eight years during which he had two legs. They shared a very special bond. She felt proud that she was able to help a very old man. He kept a very special smile for the young girl who walks with joyful and energetic steps, the prosthesis removing all barriers from her path.

Hedy J. Dalin

Remember, we all stumble, every one of us. That's why it's a comfort to go hand in hand.

Emily Kimbrough

C.O.D.—Courage On Demand

In the summer of 1991, my husband and I were vacationing in Ireland. Being good American tourists, we naturally visited the Blarney Castle. And of course when you visit the Blarney Castle, you kiss the Blarney Stone. Well, to get to the Blarney Stone, you have to walk up several flights of narrow stairs. I have always had a fear of heights and am very claustrophobic, so I told my husband to go without me and let me know if he thought I could do it. When my husband got back I asked him, "Well, what do you think? Do you think I can do it?" and before he could answer, two little old ladies came up to me and said, "Honey, if we can do it, *you* can do it!" So, I kissed the Blarney Stone!

About a month after I returned from Ireland, I found out I had breast cancer. I needed radiation and chemotherapy. The doctor was obligated to tell me all the things that might happen to me as a result of the chemotherapy. He said I might lose my hair, I might become violently sick to my stomach, I might have severe diarrhea, I might run a high fever, my jaw might lock and so on. Then he asked, "Are you ready to start?" Oh, yeah! I really felt ready to start now!

While my husband and I were sitting in the waiting room, waiting for my treatment, I became very anxious and scared. I turned to him and said, "Do you think I can do this?" Sitting across from us were two little old ladies who had just completed their chemo treatment! My husband took my hand and said, "Doll, this is going to be just like the Blarney Castle! If they can do it, *you* can do it!" *And I did it!*

Do you know the really neat thing about courage? It shows up when you need it!

Maureen Corral

The Obstacle in Our Path

In ancient times, a king had a boulder placed on a roadway. Then he hid himself and watched to see if anyone would remove the huge rock. Some of the kingdom's wealthiest merchants and courtiers came by and simply walked around it. Many loudly blamed the king for not keeping the roads clear, but none did anything about getting the big stone out of the way. Then a peasant came along, carrying a load of vegetables. On approaching the boulder, the peasant laid down his burden and tried to move the stone to the side of the road. After much pushing and straining, he finally succeeded.

As the peasant picked up his load of vegetables, he noticed a purse lying in the road where the boulder had been. The

purse contained many gold coins and a
note from the king indicating that the gold
was for the person who removed the boulder from the roadway.

The peasant learned what many others
never understand: Every obstacle presents
an opportunity to improve one's condition.

Brian Cavanaugh

When faced with
a decision—decide.
When faced with
a choice—choose.
Sitting on the fence
will leave you too tense
Because you neither
win nor lose!

Barry Spilchuk

$\overline{4}$

ON
REMEMBERING

*D*eath is not the greatest loss in
life. The greatest loss is what
dies inside us while we live.

Norman Cousins

On Your Marc . . .

Judy and Jim lost their son, Marc, more than fifteen years ago. As many parents do, Jim and Judy took for granted that both their children would outlive them. One day, Marc's life was taken suddenly by a very rare disease. There was no indication that he was sick; therefore, Judy and Jim never had the chance to say good-bye to their son and tell him how much they loved him. They were completely devastated by the loss of their son.

Many years later, Judy and Jim took a vacation to Bermuda. There they saw a beautiful statue that they both absolutely loved. The statue was of a little boy sitting on a bench reading a book. Although they were both completely drawn to the statue and wanted it dearly, it was too expensive and they could not afford it. But Jim took note of the artist's name and address anyway.

Many years later, Jim wanted to buy the statue for Judy as a surprise for her fiftieth birthday. He sought out the artist's studio but the clerk said there were only ten of those statues made in the world. The only chance of purchasing one would be if the artist would give up his own original. The artist personally contacted Jim and sadly informed him that his wife would never part with the statue. However, the artist did promise to try to locate some of the other owners to see if they were willing to part with their statue. Finally, he found a woman in England who was willing to sell her statue to Jim.

On Judy's fiftieth birthday, Jim surprised her with the statue that they fell in love with so many years before. Judy was absolutely dumbfounded. As they sat there admiring the statue, they suddenly noticed something about the statue that they hadn't noticed before. As they looked closely at the book the little boy was reading, inscribed on the cover were the words, "Book Marc." The second word was spelled M-A-R-C, just as their son spelled his name. Although Judy and Jim thought their little boy was gone forever, he managed to convey his love to both his parents on his mother's fiftiethth birthday. Our physical bond is temporary. Only love is eternal.

Denise Sasaki

Oh, How I Loved Her

The clergyman was finishing the grave-side service. Suddenly, the seventy-eight-year-old man whose wife of fifty years had just died began screaming in a thick accent, "Oh, oh, oh, how I loved her!" His mournful wail interrupted the dignified quiet of the ceremony. The other family and friends standing around the grave looked shocked and embarrassed. His grown children, blushing, tried to shush their father. "It's okay, Dad; we understand. Shush." The old man stared fixedly at the casket lowering slowly into the grave. The clergyman went on. Finishing, he invited the family to shovel some dirt onto the coffin as a mark of the finality of death. Each, in turn, did so with the exception of the old man. "Oh, how I *loved* her!" he moaned loudly. His daughter and two sons again tried to restrain him, but he continued, "I loved her!"

Now, as the rest of those gathered around began leaving the grave, the old man stubbornly resisted. He stayed, staring into the grave. The clergyman approached. "I know how you must feel, but it's time to leave. We all must leave and go on with life."

"Oh, how I loved her!" the old man moaned, miserably. "You don't understand," he said to the clergyman, "I *almost* told her once."

Hanoch McCarty, Ed.D.

The greatest weakness of most humans is their hesitancy to tell others how much they love them while they're still alive.

O. A. Battista

Merry Christmas, Jennifer

Hi, sweetheart. Christmas won't be the same without you this year, but we will try to cope with the many memories of our nineteen years spent with you. All I want for Christmas is to have you back with us, but knowing that is impossible I will settle for a letter to you: God will hopefully hand-deliver it in time for the holiday.

I missed having you being here to help me with my Christmas shopping. You always had a sense of what your mom liked. I managed okay, I think you were probably helping me. Your mom will love the gift you sent her from Heaven! Sarah, too!

You mom has done a lot of baking this week: uncooked cake, date squares, etc. Surprised, eh?

Our traditional Christmas get-together will be at your Uncle Steve's place this year. We don't know how we will handle it, but will cross that bridge when we come to it.

Sarah is doing okay, still dating Brian (which has really helped her). We know she misses you mostly at nights, when you two would do so much talking. She misses her big sister's advice and odd spat!

I have to go to the cemetery tomorrow and shovel three and one-half feet of snow, in case some of the family want to visit your grave site. We decorated the poles, hung a white and red bird and a few bells for you to hear when the wind blows. It really looks nice. We know Patrick misses you, and you him. Sorry I wasn't more supportive of your relationship; that will bother me until I can apologize in person.

I'm sorry you never got to experience the Internet, Jenny. You would have loved it! I have met some wonderful people online, families that have also lost children. They have helped me tremendously in coping with your death. Most times, other than your mom, it has been my only release. Losing one's child is the most pain a parent can experience, and being able to correspond with others in the same situation is surely a blessing. Jennifer, *we will miss you always.* We will never stop loving you or ever forget you!

Love, Sarah, Mom and Dad Furrow

Merry Christmas.
Love, Jennifer

(In the previous story, *Merry Christmas, Jennifer,* Wayne Furrow sent his departed daughter, Jennifer, a Christmas letter via the Internet. It was picked up by a few people and shortly after, Mr. Furrow received this reply.)

> *Dad,*
>
> *I did get to experience the Internet and you're right—I love it. I don't think it's the same Net you are on, though. I travel the universe—no downtime, flames, smears, nothing like that at all.*
>
> *I am with you Christmas morning. Actually, I'm with you every morning. Haven't you felt my presence? Heard my voice? Seen me in a thousand different places? I can do that for a while, but eventually I will have to spend more and*

more of my time spreading around the things you taught me: love, caring, giving, loyalty.

I can't say that I miss you because where I am there are no feelings that are sad. Honestly! Not ever! I do know when you think of me and I am happy. Did you know that I can view my whole life with you and Sarah and Mom in just a few seconds? Can you imagine?

I have so many other people here who are the greatest. Someday you'll find out for yourself. Just remember this, Daddy, I'm never sad. I have a feeling that someday this great feeling will be even greater. That's because you'll be with me. Don't be in any rush, though. There are a lot of neat things that you can do down there that I can't do up here, like love Mom a lot.

Love, Jennifer

Mr. Furrow, I lost a wife and a child a long time ago. I wish I could have received one last letter. God be with you and please forgive an old man's sentimentality. Your letter touched me at the very core of my being.

Every blessing to you.
Fr. Howard Gorle

A Child's Wisdom

I was sixteen when I met and fell in love with Bob. Two years later we married and it seemed like a fairy tale come true. A day never went by that we didn't profess our love for each other or for our three beautiful kids.

Every night as we drifted to sleep, we'd make plans for the future. But then Bob was diagnosed with leukemia—and after an eighteen-month struggle, he died at age forty-two. I felt as if I'd died, too.

That night, friends came over to comfort me. As I forced myself to eat, the six-year-old daughter of one of my husband's close friends asked, "Miss Alice, are you getting another husband?"

"Hailey!" someone admonished, but as I looked into her wide eyes, I realized she only wanted me to be happy again.

"When you've had the best husband in the world," I sighed, "you don't want another one."

But three years later, I had to tell Hailey there were two "best" husbands—when I married her father, Mark, who brought joy back into my life. Hailey's fifteen now, and we still smile over her innocent question, which was a very wise way of reminding me life has a wonderful way of going on.

Alice Cravens Moore
Excerpted from Woman's World

Children reinvent your world for you.

Susan Sarandon

Reminder

On December 24, the evening of my father's funeral, my siblings and I gathered together in our childhood home to decide where our mother would live. My father left behind five children and my mother, the love of his life for fifty-four years. She was barely able to walk or function and he had been her devoted helper. She could not live alone.

We began to talk, and as Mother listened, the discussion quickly turned heated. With our thinking clouded by shock, our bonds loosened by our recent loss, the talk turned more to the cost of caring for Mother than to the quality of her care. As we began to argue, our pain deepened and our loss was compounded by the thought of losing each other. Mother listened in shock, and we feared the family would die with Dad.

At the height of the battle, we heard the sound of caroling, followed by a knock on the door. My brother went to open it and, grateful for the respite, we all got up to see. Outside, the lawn and porch were filled with young carolers. And leading them was the priest who that day had buried Dad. He was as surprised to see us as we were to see him. He did not know that this was my parents' house.

We stood chastened by the sounds of "Peace on Earth," then closed the door. My oldest brother, stunned by the sound, whispered: "Dad sent them. He's reminding us to behave ourselves and take care of our mother."

With those words echoing in our minds, the arguments ceased, and within hours, we had decided on a plan. Our mother would move in with one of my brothers. The house of our youth was closed and bare, but the family was furnished anew.

Marilyn L. Teplitz

My Own Personal Hero

Uncle Gordyn had always been my own personal hero. When I was six years old, he scraped the mud off my dress shoes so I wouldn't get in trouble. During my freshman year, Mom and I constantly battled over whether I had to wear her old, outgrown nylons with ugly seams to school. The subject was never mentioned again after my uncle sided with me. When my parents bought my younger brother, but not me, a car, he righted that injustice, too.

But what I loved most about him was how he always had the ability to make me feel like I was the most precious being in the entire world. When my parents were planning their fiftieth wedding anniversary, he told them that he wouldn't attend. Although it had been twenty years since he and my aunt divorced, the thought of facing the entire family and their disapproval was too much for him. Even though he always said no, Mom kept asking if he would come. Finally, he told her *not* to ask again. When he did show up at the party, I told him that every time I called Mom, I asked if he was coming. "I know, honey," he said, "that's why I came." I would forever be his little princess.

When he passed away, I thought, "I'm sad because I'll never have another Christmas with him." But somehow my grief went deeper than that. In one swift and profound insight, it came to me that although the grown-up me had many loving, accepting friends, the six-year-old inside me, who had felt rejected and unloved as a child, no longer had anyone who saw her as a princess, and I desperately needed that.

One night in a dream, I saw Uncle Gordyn swinging the six-year-old in his arms. "I did both," he said to the grown-up me. "Now it's your turn." I told him I didn't understand. "All these years you didn't love yourself," he said, "so I had to love you enough for me and for you. I did both. Now it's your turn." And in my heart, I gathered little Nancy in my arms and whispered, "You're my little princess." The look in her eyes was one I had seen before—it's the look a little girl gives to her own personal hero.

Nancy Richard-Guilford

Big B

I nicknamed him Big B; he was my older brother. We were total opposites and drove each other crazy, but we also shared much, creating an unbreakable bond between us. We both knew what it was like to believe that nothing we did, no matter how hard we tried, felt like it was good enough. Everyone who knew Big B adored him. He had a huge heart and believed in everyone else's goodness—except his own.

Big B tutored hundreds of kids who had been labeled by society as stupid, lazy, undisciplined or mentally challenged. My brother saw within them an ability to make a difference. He himself had a learning disability; it was his secret. Together, he and his students knew what it felt like to be different in a world that had yet to understand.

In the last year of Big B's life he had another challenge to face, his absolute refusal to believe he was worthy of love. Big B was a beacon of light to all he touched and everybody knew it—everybody but him.

I was determined to prove to him that he was worthy of love. As cancer ravaged his body for the sixth and last time, he finally allowed me to enter his world of pain and confusion. During the last weeks of his life, only eighty pounds remained of his once 190-pound frame. His eyelids would not close, he was too weak to blink and his voice was a whisper. All I could do was hold him in my arms and love him. All he could do was accept it.

Big B was pampered around the clock and he came to love that. When he was too weak to talk, he would tap his fingers to motion me to hold his hand. My brother finally knew how to ask for and receive love! Decades of fights, misunderstandings and the helplessness of each feeling the other was unreachable had vanished. In the end, he totally surrendered to the wisdom of a higher power to help him understand the strange concept of self-love.

During one of our last conversations he secretly whispered to me, "I really am loved, aren't I?" It was the missing piece to his life's puzzle. He finally realized that he had the right to be loved.

Paula Petrovic

The "Calling Card"

My brother, Dave, was always close to our grandmother. Both of them shared a love of Mother Nature and of food that they had grown themselves. Whenever his schedule permitted, he would drop in for a short visit and a cup of coffee. One day, when he found no one home, he left a chunk of dirt on her porch. This started what was later to be known as his "calling card." Grandmother would come home occasionally and instantly know that Dave had been by when she spotted the chunk of dirt on her porch.

Although Grandmother had a poor upbringing in Italy, she managed to do well in the United States. She was always healthy and independent and enjoyed a fulfilling life. Recently, she had a stroke and died. Everyone was saddened by her death.

Dave was disconsolate. His lifelong friend was now gone.

At her funeral, Dave and I were among the grandsons who were pallbearers. At the cemetery, we were instructed by the funeral director to place our white gloves and the carnation we wore during the ceremony on our grandmother's casket. One by one, each grandson paid his final respects. Dave went before me and as he walked over to her casket, I saw him quickly lean over to pick up something. I couldn't see what it was, so I didn't pay too much attention to it. As I went to place my gloves and carnation next to Dave's, tears suddenly filled my eyes as I focused on the chunk of dirt that lay on top of my grandmother's casket. He had left his "calling card" for the final time.

Steve Kendall

Absence, like death, sets a seal on the image of those we have loved.
Goldsmith

My Father

My father had given me so much, in so many ways, and now I wanted to give something to him. How about the 100-meter gold medal from 1984? It is the one thing I could give him to represent all the good things we did together, all the positive things that had happened to me because of him.

I had never before taken any of my medals out of the bank vault where I kept them. But that day, on the way to the airport, I stopped at the bank to get the medal, and I put it in the pocket of my suit jacket. I would take it to New Jersey—for Dad.

The day of the funeral, when our family was viewing the body, I pulled out the medal to place in my father's hand. My mother asked me if I was sure I wanted to bury the medal, and I was. It would be my father's forever. "But I'm going to get another one," I told my mother. Turning to my father, I said, "Don't worry. I'm going to get another one." That was a promise—to myself and to Dad. He was lying there so peacefully, his hands resting on his chest. When I placed the medal in his hand, it fit perfectly.

Carl Lewis

The more we give of anything, the more we shall get back.

Grace Speare

Timely Departure

To look at him you would think he was a pauper. When you got to know him he was really a prince. Every day he would walk, actually shuffle, his way down to the stock-broker's office to visit his friends and watch his investments. Every afternoon at about two o'clock, Billy would walk through the door and bring a smile to our faces. His cap was always on crooked, and he always wore his worn and torn overcoat regardless of the temperature, with a scarf in the winter and a buttoned-up shirt in the summer, and always a smile (crooked teeth and all).

He was our unofficial leader, our spokes-person. If Billy said it was so, then it was *so!* We were a handful of guys getting together every day to watch the stock ticker and wait for Billy's daily words of wisdom. With his cockney accent and his reassuring wink, he seemed to make everything seem okay no matter how the market was doing or how gloomy things seemed in the real world. Then, one day, everything wasn't all right. Our Billy, our eighty-year-old pal, our leader, had cancer!

It didn't seem to matter anymore that his investments would go unwatched. What was important was that we watched Billy. He was going fast. The only family he had was an older sister in England so we became his family. A few of us took turns sitting with him in the hospital. Garry, who was Billy's friend and financial advisor, took the lead watch. Garry was there almost all the time. We didn't want Billy to be alone.

One evening, we knew the end was near. I offered to spend the night and sit with Garry and Billy, but Garry said to go home and that I could relieve him in the morning.

About 5:00 A.M. my wife and I were awakened by a loud knock on our front door. I got up to see who it was, and no one was there. At 9:00 A.M. Garry called to say that Billy had passed away during the night. "What time did he say good-bye?" I asked.

"Five o'clock A.M.," was his shocking reply. The only explanation we had for the knock on our door at 5:00 A.M. was that Billy had "winked" good-bye for one last time!

Barry Spilchuk

The Legacy

When my husband, Bob, died very suddenly in January 1994, I received condolences from people I hadn't heard from in years: letters, cards, flowers, calls, visits. I was overwhelmed with grief, yet uplifted by this outpouring of love from family, friends and even mere acquaintances.

One message touched me profoundly. I received a letter from my best friend from sixth grade through high school. We had drifted somewhat since graduation in 1949, as she stayed in our hometown and I had not. But it was the kind of friendship that could quickly resume even if we lost touch for five or ten years.

Her husband, Pete, had died perhaps twenty years ago at a young age, leaving her with deep sorrow and heavy responsibilities: finding a job and raising three young children. She and Pete, like Bob and I, had shared one of those rare, close, "love-of-your-life-you-can-never-forget" relationships.

In her letter she shared an anecdote about my mother (now long deceased). She wrote, "When Pete died, your dear mother hugged me and said, 'Trudy, I don't know what to say . . . so I'll just say I love you.'"

She closed her letter to me repeating my mother's words of so long ago, "Bonnie, I don't know what to say . . . so I'll just say I love you."

I felt I could almost hear my mother speaking to me now. What a powerful message of sympathy! How dear of my friend to cherish it all those years and then pass it on to me. I love you. Perfect words. A gift. A legacy.

Bonnie J. Thomas

5

ON
ATTITUDE

A happy person is not a person in a certain set of circumstances, but rather a person with a certain set of attitudes.

Hugh Downs

Allan M. Hirsh Cartoons. *Reprinted with permission. Allan M. Hirsh.*

*You live longer
once you realize
that any time spent
being unhappy
is wasted.*

Ruth E. Renkl

Don't Punish Every Mistake

In one of my assignments as a young infantry officer, I was sent to the 48th Infantry near Frankfurt, Germany. In those days our prize weapon was a huge 280-mm atomic cannon. Guarded by infantry platoons, these guns were hauled around the forests on trucks to keep the Soviets from guessing their locations.

One day Captain Tom Miller assigned my platoon to guard a 280. I alerted my men, loaded my .45-caliber pistol and jumped into my jeep. I had not gone far when I realized that my .45 was gone.

I was petrified. In the army, losing a weapon is serious business. I had no choice but to radio Captain Miller and tell him. "You what?" he said in disbelief. He paused a few seconds, then added, "All right, continue the mission."

When I returned, uneasily contemplating my fate, Miller called me over. "I've got something for you," he said, handing me the pistol. "Some kids in the village found it where it fell out of your holster."

"Kids found it?" I felt a cold chill.

"Yeah," he said. "Luckily they only got off one round before we heard the shot and took the gun away." The disastrous possibilities left me limp. "For God's sake, son, don't let that happen again."

He drove off. I checked the magazine and found it was full. The gun had not been fired. Later I learned that I had dropped it in my tent before I ever got started. Miller had fabricated the scene about the kids to give me a good scare.

Today, the army might hold an investigation, call in lawyers and likely enter a bad mark on my record. Miller gave me the chance to learn from my mistake. His example of intelligent leadership was not lost on me. Nobody ever got to the top without slipping up. When someone stumbles, I don't believe in stomping on him. My philosophy is: "Pick 'em up, dust 'em off and get 'em moving again."

Colin Powell

Total Support!

Our friend H. Stephen Glenn is one of the most affirming, empowering individuals we have ever met. He instantly inspires us to always look for the positive.

Stephen was at his grandson's T-ball game a while back. A little boy came up to bat. He swatted the ball off the tee and ran as fast as he could to third base. The coach went up to the little boy and said, "Boy, you sure hit that ball a long way."

The little boy said, "I did?"

"Yeah, and you ran really fast to third base and surprised the heck out of everybody!"

"I did?" he asked.

"Yes, you did. I have one question to ask you before you come to the dugout to watch the rest of the inning," the coach said to the boy. "When you made the decision to run to third base instead of first, what were you thinking of?"

The boy replied, "Well, everybody that was running to first was getting put out."

The coach took the boy to the dugout to talk to him. "Last time you made the choice of running to third base instead of first, surprised everybody, and made it, but you didn't get a chance to score. Now you've got the same choice again. You can choose to run to third and probably make it okay but you won't get to score, or you can take the risk of running to first base. You may get put out, but if you make it you get a chance to score. But, whatever you decide, I want you to know we're right there behind you."

Jack Canfield and Mark Victor Hansen

Great Expectations

Pete Rose, the famous baseball player, and I have never met, but he taught me something so valuable that it changed my life.

Pete was being interviewed in spring training the year he was about to break Ty Cobb's all time hits record. One reporter blurted out, "Pete, you only need seventy-eight hits to break the record. How many at-bats do you think you'll need to get the seventy-eight hits?"

Without hesitation, Pete just stared at the reporter and very matter-of-factly said, "seventy-eight." The reporter yelled back, "Ah, come on Pete, you don't expect to get seventy-eight hits in seventy-eight at-bats do you?"

Mr. Rose calmly shared his philosophy with the throngs of reporters who were anxiously awaiting his reply to this seemingly boastful claim. "Every time I step up to the plate, I *expect* to get a hit! If I don't *expect* to get a hit, I have no right to step in the batter's box in the first place!"

"If I go up *hoping* to get a hit," he continued, "then I probably don't have a prayer to get a hit. It is a positive expectation that has gotten me all of the hits in the first place."

When I thought about Pete Rose's philosophy and how it applied to everyday life, I felt a little embarrassed. As a business person, I was *hoping* to make my sales quotas. As a father, I was *hoping* to be a good dad. As a married man, I was *hoping* to be a good husband.

The truth was that I was an adequate salesperson, I was a not-so-bad father, and I was an okay husband. I immediately decided that being okay was not enough! I wanted to be a great salesperson, a great father and a great husband. I changed my attitude to one of positive expectation, and the results were amazing. I was fortunate enough to win a few sales trips, I won Coach of the Year in my son's baseball league and I share a loving relationship with my wife, Karen, with whom I *expect* to be married to for the rest of my life! Thanks, Mr. Rose!

Barry Spilchuk

My First Kiss, and Then Some

I was a very shy teenager and so was my first boyfriend. We had been dating for about six months; this included a lot of sweaty handholding, actually watching movies, and talking about nothing in particular. We often came close to kissing and we both knew that we wanted to be kissed, but neither of us had the courage to make the first move.

Finally, while sitting on my living room couch, he decided to go for it. We talked about the weather (really), then he leaned forward. I put a pillow up to my face to block him! He kissed the pillow. I wanted to be kissed so badly, but I was too nervous to let him get close, so I moved away from him. He moved closer. We talked about the movie (who cared!), and he leaned forward again. I blocked him again!

I moved to the end of the couch. He followed, we talked. He leaned, I stood up! I walked over near the front door and stood there, leaned against the wall with my arms crossed and said impatiently, "Well, are you going to kiss me or not?" "Yes," he said. So I stood tall, closed my eyes, puckered my lips and faced upwards. I waited and waited. Why wasn't he kissing me? So I opened my eyes and he was coming right at me. I smiled. *He kissed my teeth!* I could have died. He left.

Word must have gotten around school. I never had another date all through high school. The first year away at college, I was determined to learn how to kiss with grace and confidence. I did.

In the spring, I went home to see my friends. I walked into the latest hangout and who do you suppose I saw sitting at the bar but my old kissing partner. Well, I was going to show him the new me. I walked over to his bar stool and tapped him on the shoulder. Without hesitation, I took him in my arms, dipped him back over his stool, and kissed him with my most assertive kiss. I sat him up, looked at him victoriously, and said, "So there!"

He pointed to the woman next to him and said, "Mary Jane, I'd like you to meet my wife."

Mary Jane West-Delgado

A Picture's Worth . . .

A little old man came into the store hold-ing a torn, green, vinyl double picture frame with pictures of a young couple inside. The frame had been damaged and was torn down the center. It looked like someone had tried to repair it by using stiff, letter clicker tape, which was unsuccessful. In fear of causing more damage, the man brought it to the frame shop. The expert framer was not able to repair the frame. I could not help but overhear the request, and I asked if I might take a look at the frame. I was not really sure what I was going to do, but I asked him if I could keep the picture frame overnight. The man sighed and said yes. He bowed his head as he walked out the door.

I carefully removed the stiff tape and glued the fragments back together. Next, I applied an artificial binding and cosmetically repaired the outer surface with a little bias tape and DMC floss.

The next day, the little old man came into the store and I handed him the frame. As I looked at him I said, "No charge." I paid for the supplies out of my own pocket. He was impressed by the craftsmanship and he started to cry. The pictures were of him and his wife. He pointed to the picture and said, "This is my wife; she just passed away. She put this frame together in the 1920s and I was so afraid it was ruined." As a result, tears came to my eyes and I said, "Well, you come back to see us anytime." As he walked out the door, he said, "I will never forget you, Christine."

He walked into my life at a time I was feeling uncertain about my job and I wanted to quit. He made me realize where I needed to be and what purpose my life really held. It is so much of a blessing to give from the heart. What that little old man did for me meant more to me than I could ever express. Later that year, I was quickly promoted to a high-paying position as a craft coordinator. Sometimes, God brings people into our lives for a reason. I don't even know his name, but I will never forget my little picture-frame man.

Christine James

Service with a Smile

Everything I learned about selling I learned in one afternoon from my father, Walt, at his furniture store in New Era, Michigan. I was twelve years old.

I was sweeping the floor when an elderly woman entered the store. I asked Dad if I could wait on her. "Sure," he replied.

"May I help you?"

"Yes, young man. I bought a sofa from your store and the leg fell off. I want to know when you're going to fix it."

"When did you purchase it, ma'am?"

"About ten years ago."

I told my father that she thought we were going to fix her old sofa for free. He said to tell her we'd be there that afternoon.

After screwing on the new leg, we left, and on the ride back Pop asked, "What's bothering you, son?"

"You know that I want to go to college. If we drive around fixing old sofas for free, we'll go broke!"

"You had to learn how to do that repair job anyway. Besides, you missed the most important part. You didn't notice the store tag when we flipped the couch over. She bought it from Sears."

"You mean we did that job for nothing and she's not even our customer?"

Dad looked me in the eye and said, "She is now."

Two days later she returned to our store and bought several thousand dollars worth of new furniture from me. When we delivered it, she put a gallon jar filled with change, singles, fives, tens, twenties, fifties and hundreds on the kitchen table. "Take what you need," she said and left the room.

I've been selling for thirty years since that day. I have had the highest closing average in every organization I have represented because I treat every customer with respect.

Michael T. Burcon

Dylan Helps Out

Two-year-old Dylan was helping me make a Jell-O dessert for a committee meeting at my home later that day. We selected a recipe that used soda pop for part of the liquid. Dylan was absolutely delighted by the sparkle and bubbling of the mixture as we poured in the pop. I left him to view the magic while I took a two-minute phone call. When I returned, I found Dylan exclaiming with glee, "Fizzie! Dylan make Fizzie!"

Fizzies are flavored tablets that create a drink of that same flavor when placed in water. The pleasure of their taste is second to that of the visual show they put on as they sizzle and bubble. I was fascinated by them as a child and was ecstatic when I found some for Dylan. "Yes," I agreed, "it does look a lot like when we make Fizzies."

Immensely proud of his assistance,

Dylan announced to each arriving guest, "Dylan make Fizzie!" Asked about the preparation process, I explained while the guests began eating the dessert. Just as I finished, Dylan's grandfather walked in and said, "Excuse me for interrupting. I can't find my denture tablet. I put it out in the kitchen this morning and now it's gone."

At that moment, Dylan let out an ear-piercing, "Dylan make Fizzie!" I looked at the dessert. I looked at Dylan. I thought of the implications. *Dear God, I just fed denture tablets to my guests.*

Unfortunately, my guests also made the same realization. I was surrounded by a room full of desperate guests—some of whom were suddenly nauseous—politely trying to spit out a mouth full of Jell-O. It wasn't pretty.

The story does have a happy ending. I have a very busy schedule, and since the "Fizzie Incident," I have never once been asked to prepare food for a committee meeting!

Nancy Richard-Guilford

Something to Look Forward To

A while ago, I was treated to a couple of pampering weeks in the beautiful mountains of Santa Barbara, California. I had asked my friends if I could stay in their guest house for the time I was finishing a book I was working on.

My first three days were incredible and I was treated to two very special things on each of those days. First, the heavens opened up and we were deluged with three days of uninterrupted rain. It was really quite cozy but after a while, I had thoughts of building an ark.

My second treat came in the form of an assistant. Every day at noon, my friends' son, Christopher, would come home from his kindergarten class and offer to "help" me. On the last day of the downpour he asked me why it was raining so much. Just to make conversation, I said, "Sometimes when it rains, it means that God is sad and he is crying."

"He's probably crying because Valentine's Day is over," explained my five-year-old prophet. In his very self-assured way he went out into the rain, looked up and said, "Don't worry, God. Valentine's Day may be over, but Easter is coming soon!"

It wasn't long after that the rain stopped!

Barry Spilchuk

"I wish God wouldn't wash the
world on Saturdays."

Giving from the Heart

When I was a teenager, probably about thirteen, my mother taught me a very valuable lesson I've never forgotten. We were grocery shopping in a small store one day when I noticed a family come into the store. It looked like a mother, her daughter, and her granddaughter. They were clean but dressed in worn clothes, and it was obvious they were less fortunate. They pushed a cart through the store, carefully selecting items, mostly generic, and all necessary foods.

My mother and I finished our shopping and headed toward the clerk to pay. As we got there, the family was in front of us, with one person in between. As I watched the family place groceries on the conveyor belt, I heard the mother ask the clerk every so often to subtotal, as she only had so much to spend. This took a while, and the person in front of me was getting noticeably impatient and even started mumbling things which I'm sure were overheard. When the store clerk did a final total, the woman did not have enough money, so she began pointing to different food items to put back. My mother reached in her purse, pulled out a twenty dollar bill and handed it to the woman. The woman looked very surprised and said, "I can't take that!" My mother looked directly at the woman and quietly replied, "Yes, you most certainly can. Consider it a gift. There's nothing in that cart you don't really need, so please accept it." The woman then reached out and took the money, squeezing my mom's hand for just a moment, and with tears running down her cheeks, said, "Thank you very much. No one's ever done nothin' like this for me before."

I know I left the store with tears in my eyes, and it is something I will cherish forever. You see, my parents raised six children and didn't have a whole lot of money themselves, although I can never remember wanting for anything. I'm very happy to say that I inherited her caring heart. I have given selflessly before, and there is not a better feeling in the whole world!

Dee M. Taylor

Rock Concert

Even without the torn jeans, he made a scruffy-looking ten year old. His fifth grade classmates had never seen anyone as poorly dressed and unpolished as Marco. This was his first day of elementary school in a quaint New England town of well-to-do families. Marco's parents were migrant fruit pickers and his classmates eyed him with suspicion for the first part of the day. Even though they whispered and made comments about his clothes, he didn't seem to notice.

Then came recess and the kickball game. Marco led off the first inning with a home run, earning him a bit of respect from his wardrobe critics. Next up to kick was Richard, the least athletic and most overweight child in the class. After his second strike (amid the groans of his classmates),

Marco edged up to Richard and quietly said, "Forget them, kid. You can do it!" Richard kicked a home run and at that precise moment, something began to change in Marco's class. Over the next few months, Marco was able to teach the class many new things. Things such as how to tell when fruit was ripe, how to call a wild turkey and, especially, how to treat other people.

By the time Marco's parents finished their work in the area, the class was preparing to celebrate Christmas. While other students brought the teacher fancy scarves, perfumes and soaps, Marco stepped up to the teacher's desk with a special gift. It was a rock, which was beautiful and bright, that he delivered into the teacher's hands. "I polished it up special," he said.

Years later, the teacher still had Marco's rock on her desk. At the beginning of each school year, she would tell her class about the gentle boy who taught her and her class not to judge a book by its cover. And that it's what's on the inside of others that truly counts.

This Little Light of Mine

Hold Your Tongue

Ida and David both wanted all their sons to graduate from college. They knew their boys would have to pay their own way since David never made more than $150 a month. Still, they encouraged their sons to achieve all they could. Arthur, however, went directly from high school to a job. Edgar began studying law. When Dwight graduated, he didn't have a goal in mind, so he and Ed made a pact: Dwight would work two years while Ed studied, sending Ed as much as he could, and then they would reverse the arrangement. While working, Dwight found an opportunity that appealed to him more than college—West Point.

Both Ida and David were crushed by Dwight's decision. Ida was deeply convinced that soldiering was wicked. Still, all she ever said to him was, "It is your choice." David also remained silent, allowing his adult son full freedom to forge his own future.

Yes, Ida and David wisely held their tongues—but they never withheld their applause, especially on the day their son, General Dwight Eisenhower, became president of the United States of America.

God's Little Devotional Book

*The thing always
happens that you really
believe in; and the belief
in a thing makes
it happen.*

Frank Lloyd Wright

$\overline{6}$

EVERYDAY HEROES

The measure of a man's real character is what he would do if he knew he would never be found out.

T. B. Macaulay

A Very Belated Thank-You

When my son, Mark, was in the third grade he saved all his allowance for more than two months to buy holiday presents for those he loved. He had saved twenty dollars. The third Saturday in December Mark announced that he had made his list and had his money in his pocket.

I drove him to a local drug store, the modern version of what we used to call the "Five and Dime." Mark picked up a hand basket and went off on his own while I waited patiently reading a book at the front of the store. It took Mark more than forty-five minutes to pick out his presents. The smile on his face as he approached the checkout counter was truly joyful. The clerk rang up his purchases as I politely looked the other way. Mark kept within his budget and reached into his pocket for

his money. It was not there. There was a
hole in his pocket, but no money. Mark
stood in the middle of the store holding his
basket, tears rolling down his cheeks. His
whole body was shaking with his sobs.
Then an amazing thing happened. A customer in the store came up to Mark. She
knelt down to his level and took him in her
arms and said, "You would do me the
greatest favor if you let me replace your
money. It would be the most wonderful
present you could ever give me. I only ask
that one day, you pass it on. One day,
when you are grown, I would like you to
find someone you can help. When you do
help this other person, I know you will feel
as good about it as I do now." Mark took
the money, tried to dry his tears and ran to
the check-out counter as fast as he could
go. I think we all enjoyed our gifts that
year almost as much as Mark enjoyed giving them to us.

I would like to say "thank-you" to that
incredible woman. I would like to tell her
that four years later Mark went house to
house collecting blankets and coats for the
people in the Oakland fire—and he thought
of her. I would like to tell her every time I

give food to a homeless family, I think of her. And I want to promise her that Mark will never forget to keep passing it on.

Laurie Pines

One for the Team

This story was told by an old priest one Sunday. It is a true story of when he served in the military.

One day their drill sergeant came out and threw a hand grenade into a group of young soldiers. The men all ran away and took cover away from the grenade. Then the drill sergeant told them that the grenade was not set to explode and he just did it to see their reaction. The next day a newly recruited soldier joined the group. The drill sergeant told the other soldiers not to tell the new soldier what was going to happen. As the drill sergeant came out and threw the grenade into the crowd of soldiers, the new soldier, not knowing it wasn't going to explode, threw himself on top of the grenade to prevent it from killing the other men. He was willing to die for his fellow soldiers.

That year the young man was awarded the only medal for courage and bravery that had not been won during battle.

Kim Noone

*Four things to learn in life:
To think clearly without
hurry or confusion;
To love everybody sincerely;
To act in everything with
the highest motives;
To trust God unhesitatingly.*

Helen Keller

My Daddy Is Magic!

My sister Lois was born in January so she was too young to remember her first couple of winters in Chicago. However, when she was three years old (you know, that age when you feel that your parents could, and would, do anything for you) she woke up to see that a blanket of snow had covered her world while she was asleep. This was the first time she had seen snow. She came bounding out of her bedroom into the kitchen where the rest of the family was eating breakfast and with her blue eyes opened wide she excitedly asked my father, "Daddy, how did you do that?"

John Sandquist

"God gift-wrapped the world!"

Family Circus Cartoons. *Reprinted with permission of King Features Syndicate.*

A Day at the Lake

"Me play!" said the mentally challenged boy.

"Sure," I said.

I threw him the ball.

"Yeah! Me catch!" he screamed.

"Okay, now throw it back," I said.

The boy threw it back. I caught it and dove underwater.

"You don't have to do this," said the boy's mother.

"No, it's fun," I said.

"Yeah, go under 'gain!" yelled the boy. So I dove underwater.

We continued playing for half an hour. When the boy went away he had the biggest smile I've ever seen on his face. This small experience made me feel normal. I thought that's what anyone would do. A boy wanted to play, so I did. This made the boy feel good so it made me feel good. But after that people stared at me.

One boy even came up to me and said, "Why were you playing with that retardo?!"

I said nothing and walked away.

Kevin Toole
6th Grade

*If you have one true friend
you have more than your share.*
Thomas Fuller

Welcome Home

In 1921 my grandparents emigrated from Russia due to the pogroms driving the Jews out of the country. Their emergence was adventurous in itself. Eventually they arrived at the docks. Everyone who was boarding the boats for America had to show fifty dollars before they were allowed into America. My uncle, who was in America, sent the money to my grandparents. While they were boarding the boat my grandfather noticed a little boy crying hysterically. My grandfather went over to him. The boy told my grandfather that he lost his money and would not be allowed into the country. My grandfather gave the small boy, whose name was Isadore Feterman, his fifty dollars. Once they arrived in America my grandfather had to contact my uncle and tell him that he needed more money. My grandfather had to wait several days. Eventually everyone was allowed in the United States.

Fifteen years later my grandfather was at his junk shop. A limousine pulled up and out came two men. They asked for Benjamin Lasensky. My grandfather replied that it was he. The man introduced himself as Isadore Feterman and handed a blank check to my grandfather. He said, "I owe my success and happiness in America to you. Fill the check to whatever amount you desire." (Isadore was a well-known millionaire.) My grandfather called my uncle and told him. My uncle said, "Just fill it out for the fifty dollars we gave him."

Some years passed and they lost touch again. Several years later, my grandfather's cousin was living in New York where Isadore Feterman lived. It was my grandfather's eighty-fifth birthday. My grandfather's cousin looked up Mr. Feterman and invited him to my grandfather's party. He replied, "I wouldn't miss it for the world." So, Isadore Feterman came to Grandpa's eighty-fifth birthday party and it was a pleasant surprise for my grandfather. Isadore told everyone there the story of how he came to America.

Amy Cubbison

Charity of Poor People

He was not your typical cabbie. As we took off from the downtown Hyatt en route to the Kansas City Airport, he drove by what appeared to be a sparsely furnished office in a relatively seedy section of downtown. Then he said proudly, "That's my office!" The window front said "COPP" on it. He said, "I take care of the invisible ten thousand Kansas City homeless out of there." I could sense the emotion in his words. My eyes started tearing up.

"Yep," Richard Tripp said, "I feed eight hundred people Christmas breakfast when they get kicked out of the regular shelters that are preparing for Christmas dinner. I started COPP (Charity of Poor People) when I got back on my feet again after being homeless for six months. I'd been hackin' twenty years and got too many speedin' tickets, lost my license and was suddenly homeless. It wasn't too bad. See those truckin' yards? They got heavy plastic that I pulled out of their garbage cans. Heavy duty plastic makes a rain-proof tent and sleepin' bag that'll keep you alive. I slept in those woods over there every night for six months. If someone's homeless over six months, nine out of ten of 'em will stay permanently homeless. I give 'em a new choice and a chance.

"We don't take no money—only food, long johns, and real stuff the homeless need now. I go on the radio and get lots of stuff.

"Last year a husband and wife who heard me on the radio came into COPP, and I touched 'em because I talk with my heart. The couple's five-year-old daughter got killed by a hit-and-run driver. They gave gloves to eight hundred people in memory of their daughter. It was the best and most useful gift I ever saw anyone give. Everyone thanked 'em and cried because their hands would not freeze anymore."

Because of Richard Tripp, five thousand of the ten thousand homeless people in Kansas City have been served meals and provided clothing on a yearly basis.

Mark Victor Hansen

Information Please

I used to have a job as a telephone operator. All you had to do was dial 411 and you got me. This service provides telephone numbers; however, many people think, "Gee! Information, they know everything about everything." I would get calls for, "Ya know dat girl? She live in a brown house on dat one roa? She my frien in ma class. She got brown hair." I would also get calls like, "Can you tell me how to make egg salad?"

Well, one day I got a call and it was around Christmastime. I said, "Directory assistance, may I help you?" There was a man on the phone and in a very lonely voice he said, "Ma'am, I need . . . my cat needs some food." He sounded so helpless, but I had to disconnect him. It was against the rules to give out anything other than phone numbers, so I disconnected him. He called back and by some miracle I got him again. And again, in his frail voice, he said, "Ma'am, please don't hang up on me. My poor cat . . . she's so hungry. All I want for Christmas is for her to have some food. Please, miss . . . please help me." What could I do? This poor man sounded so sincere. I had to do something! I quickly asked him for his address and took it down on a piece of paper. I told him I would see what I could do. I just knew I had to do something for this poor old man and his cat. I went to my supervisor and asked if I could take the rest of the evening off. It was getting dark out and it was starting to snow.

I left the building and went to the store. I bought a big bag of cat food, tied a big red ribbon on it and attached a card from Santa. I got the old man's address out of my pocket and went in search of his house. It was in a bad section of the city, and when I got there it was dark and snowing. I walked up to the porch and crept up the musty, creaky stairs. I set down the bag of cat food, rang the doorbell, and ran to my car and hid. I watched from my car as a wrinkly old man opened the door. The smile on his face when he saw the food and read the card was the best Christmas present I ever received!

Molly Melville

A Friend in Need

My six-year-old son, Willie, was thrilled when the tooth fairy left him a dollar.

In the morning, as Willie got ready for school, he tucked the bill in his pocket. Afraid he might lose it, I suggested he leave the money at home.

"Mom, I have to take it with me," Willie insisted. "Some of my friends don't have enough money to buy chocolate milk."

Those kids sure have a terrific friend. And Willie has one proud mom.

Mary Joy Long
Excerpted from Woman's World

*Friendship is
the golden thread that
ties the heart of all
the world.*

John Evelyn

Unfinished Business

I was home this weekend "Mom-sitting." Mom was not feeling well and needed some help. Dad works part-time, and with help from many friends and family, he helps Mom get around. This weekend, Dad told me the story behind one woman who helps. But first, you need to know a little about our house when I was growing up. My parents believed that as many of us as possible (there were eight of us kids) should get exposure to the world. Three of us were exchange students (Australia, Brazil and Holland). You'd think that this was their way of "unloading" us so as to lower the grocery bill. But, when we were gone, they'd invite other exchange students to stay with them (Australia, Holland and Japan). Mom's feeling was that it was easier to add a seventh or eighth kid in our house than it was to add a third or a fourth child in another family.

Nowadays, Mom doesn't entertain. She doesn't get around too well, so some of my brothers built a shower bath on the first floor. Every week, a nurse named Beth comes to help Mom with her bath. Dad recently told her how much she appreciated her coming, and he asked her as gently as he could why she was so committed to helping Mom. Beth answered, "Oh, I guess you don't remember. I was your 'exchange' student from Williams Street when I was first born. You took me in as a newborn for four months when my mother was sick. It's great to be able to pay you back."

Mike Lynott

*B*eing considerate of others will take your children further in life than any college degree.

Marian Wright Edelman

Making Change

A young boy went to a police department auction of bicycles accumulated over a period of time. Each time the auctioneer started the bidding, the boy would say, "I bid one dollar, sir." The bidding would continue higher and higher until each bicycle was sold to the highest bidder. Each time the boy would bid one dollar. As the last bicycle to be sold was brought forth, the little boy cried out, "I bid one dollar, sir." The figures in the bidding rose higher and the auctioneer finally closed the bidding at nine dollars to the little boy in the front row.

Then the auctioneer reached into his pocket and pulled out eight dollars and laid them on the counter; the little boy came up and put his one dollar in nickels, dimes and pennies alongside it, picked up his new bike, and started out the door. Then he laid the bike down, ran back to the auctioneer and threw his arms around the auctioneer's neck and cried.

Elder Featherstone
Submitted by Jack ZoBell

If you want happiness . . .
For an hour—take a nap
For a day—go fishing
For a month—get married
For a year—inherit a fortune
For a lifetime—
help someone else.

Chinese proverb

Living Example

Reporters and city officials gathered at a Chicago railroad station one afternoon in 1953. The person they were meeting was the 1952 Nobel Peace Prize winner. A few minutes after the train came to a stop, a giant of a man—six feet, four inches—with bushy hair and a large mustache stepped from the train. Cameras flashed. City officials approached him with hands outstretched. Various people began telling him how honored they were to meet him.

The man politely thanked them and then, looking over their heads, asked if he could be excused for a moment. He quickly walked through the crowd until he reached the side of an elderly black woman who was struggling with two large suitcases. He picked up the bags and with a smile, escorted the woman to a bus. After helping her aboard, he wished her a safe journey. As he returned to the greeting party he apologized, "Sorry to have kept you waiting."

The man was Dr. Albert Schweitzer, the famous missionary doctor who had spent his life helping the poor in Africa. In response to Schweitzer's action, one member of the reception committee said with great admiration to the reporter standing next to him, "That's the first time I ever saw a sermon walking."

God's Little Devotional Book

There are two ways of spreading light: to be the candle or the mirror that receives it.

Edith Wharton

7

ECLECTIC
WISDOM

Kindness is the inability to remain at ease in the presence of another person who is ill at ease, the inability to remain comfortable in the presence of another who is uncomfortable, the inability to have peace of mind when one's neighbor is troubled.

Rabbi Samuel H. Holdenson

The Beholder's Eye

Shoving the vacuum into its home in the hall closet, I stifled a groan. A half-day of housework behind me and I still wasn't ready for the out-of-state company expected any minute. My four small children whirled through, leaving a wake of toys, crumbs and stray shoes scattered across the recently trackless carpet. And then I saw it: the sliding doors of the family room. The ones I had washed and scrubbed earlier that morning. Generous finger streaks and tiny nose prints mottled the freshly polished glass panes. *And that looks like . . .* Frowning, I stepped nearer and bent for a closer inspection. *Why, it is! Peanut butter and Oreo cookies smudged all over. Those kids!* Near tears, I plopped onto the couch and grabbed the jangling phone. "Hello?" I growled.

"Hello, dear," answered my mother from her own couch a state away. "Are you busy?"

"Oh, you have no idea!" I said, exasperated. "We're expecting guests, and I just can't seem to get all the housework caught up around here, and the kids . . ."

"That reminds me," she interrupted. "I should do some of my own. Housework, that is. The mirror above the couch is smeared. But, you know, every time I look at the sweet baby prints your little ones left there last month, I can't bring myself to wipe them away. After all, I'm still showing them off to my friends as 'priceless artwork'!" My gaze ping-ponged around the room. A half-eaten cracker here, wadded socks there, tilting towers of picture books in the corner. I grinned. Crowning it all was a hand-painted masterpiece on the patio doors. Unnumbered. One-of-a-kind. My own piece of priceless artwork.

Carol McAdoo Rehme

Worry is an abuse of God's gift of imagination.

Corrine Lajeunesse

Allan M. Hirsh Cartoons. *Reprinted with permission. Allan M. Hirsh.*

*When you come to
the edge of all the light you
know, and are about to
step off into the darkness of
the unknown, faith is
knowing one of two things
will happen: There will be
something solid to stand
on or you will be taught
how to fly.*

Barbara J. Winter

Dream Weaver

"That one's for you, Daddy!" yelled Matthew Ryan Emrich, not yet nine, looking to the sky, as he circled the bases with his fist held high. Matthew had just hit his first home run as a member of his Little League team—a grand slam on his "Field of Dreams!"

His father, Mark, had always wanted to be a professional baseball player. He tried out and survived several "cuts," but never lived his dream—a dream instilled and supported by his father, Chet.

Mark continued to play on sandlot teams and taught neighborhood children how to play. When Matthew was born on July 30, 1985, Mark promised himself he would share his dream with his son. By the time Matthew was four, he was hitting a baseball over the neighbor's roof.

Matthew's uniform number—7—was the same as his father's. He was so pleased that his daddy loved him as he enjoyed the family tradition. After all, the movie "Field of Dreams," is not just about baseball—it's about fathers and sons and it's about faith!

Sadly, yet with great faith, Mark bravely faced, but lost, a hard-fought battle with cancer. He was thirty-three. The Sunday that Mark died, he had entered the hospital for "observation only." The doctors had promised that he could be released to see Matthew's first game on Monday afternoon.

Family and friends knew that Matthew would play the next day, just as his father would have wished. Little did Matthew know that the promise he had made to his mother, Sherry, that "my first ball will be hit for my daddy," would be heard by a much higher, ever-present power.

The comment that Matthew's achievement "probably knocked his father off the cloud from which he was watching" sums up the victories of this life for all of us, doesn't it?

Ronald D. Eberhard

Ministering Angel

One night in September 1977, Ann and Gary Cannady of Fayetteville, North Carolina, were visited by what they say was a genuine angel. At their door was a very tall black man with brilliant blue eyes, who said, "God sent me to tell Ann a message. Her cancer is gone."

They were dumbfounded. For weeks they had been praying that Ann would be cured of her uterine cancer and thus spared a radical hysterectomy. Ann asked, "Who are you? How do you know my name?" The stranger said his name was Thomas, quoted Bible passages, then raised his right hand toward Ann to pray. Sensing an intense heat, she suddenly collapsed. When she came to, Thomas was gone.

On her demand, Ann's doctor performed another biopsy. He found no sign of disease—and she has been cancer-free ever since. The experience led Ann, now sixty-one, to open a shop of angel collectibles. "God healed me," she says, "but Thomas was his messenger."

Ladies' Home Journal

*God enters by a private door
into every individual.*

Ralph Waldo Emerson

Passing the Test

It was 5:30 A.M. in May of 1947. I was eating a bowl of cold cereal and a slice of toast in the parsonage kitchen in a little town twenty miles east of Des Moines, Iowa. All night I had been wrestling with and praying about a dilemma. I still owed $50 on my tuition at Drake University and today began the finals for my senior year. Rules of the business office stated that all tuition and fees must be paid before prospective graduates would be allowed to take their final exams. Dare I write a "hot" check? Where would I get the money to cover it?

My wife and I had married in my freshman year and by the end of my sophomore year our first child was born. Now we had two boys and my wife had undergone surgery the past summer. As student pastor in this small-town church we were privileged to live in the parsonage and receive a small salary. To supplement our income I had worked after school hours and Saturdays at the *Des Moines Register and Tribune.* Now I was so close to the end of the struggle—but yet so far.

Just then the phone rang. It was Ed, the church treasurer. "I hated to call at this early hour, but last night I got to thinkin'. We've been takin' up a little collection among the members to give to you at the time of your graduation, and I got to thinkin' maybe you needed that now, and knowin' you go into class early I thought I'd better call."

My heart leaped. "Ed," I said, "you've been thinking right and you must be an answer to my prayer. Do I ever need it now! I still have a tuition payment that has to be in before I start taking finals today."

"Well, I'll be right over." Ed was soon at my door. I thanked him for the envelope he handed me and stepped into my car to head to the university. As I pulled out onto the street, I opened the envelope and looked inside at the assortment of bills. When I counted them, it was exactly $50!

N. Gayle Fischer

And She Did It with Grace!

Saying grace at mealtime was a tradition at Grandma's house. At breakfast, lunch and supper, all who gathered around the table would bow their heads to give blessing for the food they were about to eat.

Much to Grandma's sadness, this tradition was not brought to our home by my mother, so as a three-year-old, the practice of saying grace was very confusing to me.

Mother embarrassingly recalls that once, while Grandma rambled through one of her lengthy mealtime thanks to God, I asked in a rather loud voice, "Why is Grandma talking to her plate?"

Glen DeVuono

"I know why we say grace.
It's to let our food cool off."

Wrong Number?

My mother recently passed away, after nearly a year of getting worse, recovering and getting worse again. Her life had not been much of a life since Dad had died. But that last year was really tough on her. It was no fun for Marge without George. No one to live with, no one to fight with, no one to laugh with, no one to love. She had us, of course, but it just wasn't the same for her without Dad. We understood.

While in the hospital, Mom suddenly took a dramatic turn for the worse. My sister, Betsy, was notified, and left work to go straight to the hospital. Her husband, Andy, got a hieroglyphic message, tried to reach Betsy at home, was unsuccessful and decided to call the hospital directly. Andy knew that Mom was on the seventh floor. He tried to remember her room number.

7226? 7626? 7662? He decided to call the switchboard and have the hospital operator connect him. He asked for Marge Mueth— "M-U-E-T-H," he spelled it out.

"She's in room 3643," was the surprising response. "I'll connect you." Andy couldn't understand why Mom might have been moved. A man answered the phone. Andy, not recognizing the voice, was now thoroughly confused and decided he must have the wrong room after all. "Sorry," he said, "I must have the wrong room. I'm looking for the Mueth family."

The man's voice answered, "You've got 'em. This is George." Andy was completely unnerved but kept on, "No, really, I think I've got the wrong room, I'm looking for Marge Mueth." The man's voice sounded lighthearted and cheerful. "That's my wife. I'm here to pick her up."

In Andy's astonishment he hung up, called the operator again and asked for a Marge Mueth on the seventh floor. He was then connected with room 7226, and Betsy answered the phone when it rang in Mom's room.

My sister's son, Billy, summed up the situation with the simplicity and profundity that only children possess, saying, "Grandpa is here to take Grandma home." Betsy just cried and wondered out loud what had taken "Grandpa" so long.

Lin Hardick

The Luckiest Catch

Twenty-three years had passed since Eleanora Karman of North Canton, Ohio, lost her wedding ring while fishing at night.

Then last June, Eleanora, fifty-seven years old, was chatting with bingo buddy Jo Berry on their way in to the game at the local church, and Jo mentioned that she'd just caught three catfish. "If you catch a fish and find a wedding band inside, it may be mine," Eleanora joked. Her friend's face suddenly turned serious as she said, "Describe it." The white-gold ring, said Eleanora, was inscribed with the Karmans' initials and wedding date.

"I have that ring!" Jo said, and dashed home to retrieve the band she'd once found on the shore while fishing. The tearful, jubilant reunion of jewelry and owner was

witnessed by everyone at the church—
including the priest, who turned down
Eleanora's request to bless the ring. "Honey,"
he said, "that ring is already blessed!"

Ladies' Home Journal

Faith is believing
in things when common
sense tells you not to.

George Seaton

Pass It On!

In the summer of 1965, the entire family had gathered for a family reunion in Plant City, Florida. At 2:00 A.M., my grandmother woke everyone and started issuing orders to get empty Coke bottles, corks and blank paper ready. "I've received a message from God," she said. "People must hear his word." She started writing verses on the paper, while all of the grandchildren bottled and corked the passages.

That morning, everyone drove to Cocoa Beach and deposited more than two hundred bottles into the surf.

Over the years, people wrote, called and visited my grandmother, always thanking her for the scripture. She died in November 1974. In December of 1974, the last letter arrived and it stated:

Dear Mrs. Gause,

I'm writing this letter to you by candle-light. We no longer have electricity on the farm. My husband was killed in the fall when the tractor overturned on him. He left eleven children and myself behind. They're all under the age of fourteen. The bank is foreclosing; there's one loaf of bread left; there's snow on the ground; Christmas is two weeks away. I prayed to the Lord to forgive me, before I went to the river to drown myself. It's been frozen over for weeks now, so I didn't think it would take long. I had to break the ice, and as I did, a Coke bottle floated up. I opened it, and with tears and trembling hands, I read about hope. Ecclesiastes 9:4.

"But for him who is joined to all the living there is hope, for a living dog is better than a dead lion."

You went on to reference other scriptures: Hebrew 7:19, 6:18, John 3:3. I came home and read my Bible, and now I'm thanking God for the message. We're going to make it now. Please pray for us, but know we're all right.

May God bless you and yours.

A Farm in Ohio

Chrystle White

Second Chance

They say God works in mysterious ways. Sixteen-year-old James Hogan* had no idea God was about to intervene in his life. He'd dropped out of school a few weeks earlier and had a job delivering pizzas. Described by his teachers and employers as a courteous, hard worker, James just couldn't seem to handle the pressures of adolescence. His life was going nowhere fast despite the silent prayers of his mother.

Always conscientious, he delivered pizzas hot from the oven until the day he saw the back of a Cadillac sinking into a small pond. The car was going down fast with an elderly man inside. Without hesitation, James slammed his delivery truck to a stop and leaped into the water. Trapped inside was

*The names in this story have been changed.

the Reverend Max Kelly. He was uncon-
scious. James, standing on the back of the
car, saw that a rear window had somehow
opened. He pulled the elderly man out and
brought him to shore.

After the rescue, the police offered James a
ride home. He declined, stating that he had
his truck to drive and pizza to deliver. Ever
conscientious, he did ask them to radio the
restaurant to notify his customers that their
pizzas would be a little late and a little cold.

In December of 1995, James Hogan was
awarded the Carnegie Medal for heroism,
which included $2,500, a medal and a scholar-
ship. James says the incident has changed
his life. Just two weeks before the accident,
he had held a gun to his head wanting to
die. He wouldn't have been there to save
the Reverend's life had the gun not jammed.

His mother's prayers answered, James is
back in school, taking extra classes to catch
up with his classmates and practicing for
the baseball team. A huge public outpouring of love and support has given him a
renewed meaning and purpose and a well-
earned second chance.

Joanie Nietsche

God Would Have Wanted It That Way!

Never! Never did I ever think that I would lose both of my parents on the same day. However, I received a phone call telling me that both of my parents had been killed in an automobile accident.

Why did they both have to die the same day?! Why me? Why did two good people like them have to die? Why? Why? Why? Why?

I caught the next flight out to Kentucky absolutely in shock, full of questions and disbelief. I met my two sisters who were hysterical and in full denial that this could be happening to us.

I went to my parents' home and there, laying on the stand next to my dad's favorite rocking chair, was the birthday gift I had sent him. In their home, their spirit and ambiance were still warm, and it seemed to collect around me in a mysterious way. I couldn't believe it; I had talked to them only two days earlier on the phone. Now, forever gone! Eternity!

During the four-day wake, several hundred friends and relatives came to pay their respects. Friends sat around the casket recalling the good times they had with my dear parents. I was never more proud of them in my life. But the one thing that helped me understand their deaths more than anything was the statement made in the eulogy by Reverend Dewitt Furrow. He said, "You may ask why they were called to heaven on the same day! They would have wanted it that way, since they were never apart, always hand in hand and arm in arm, always walking in love on this earth. It would be selfish of us to want one to stay, one to go on. The remaining one would have died of grief within a year. God has two angels now, walking around heaven together as they did here on earth. God would have wanted it that way!"

Later, while praying and crying at the cemetery, I just stared at their graves. Then, words seemed to resound through the air

so clearly that it startled me and they were,
"God would have wanted it that way."
  He would.

Douglas Paul Blankenship

Breaking the Silence

"How did you do it, Dad? How have you managed to not take a drink for almost twenty years?" It took me almost twenty years to have the courage to even ask my father this very personal question. When Dad first quit drinking, the whole family was on pins and needles every time he got into a situation that, in the past, would have started him drinking again. For a few years we were afraid to bring it up for fear the drinking would begin again.

"I had this little poem that I would recite to myself at least four to five times a day," was Dad's reply to my eighteen-year-old unasked question. "The words were an instant relief and constant reminder to me that things were never so tough that I could not handle them," Dad said. And then he shared the poem with me. The

poem's simple, yet profound words immediately became part of my daily routine as
well.

About a month after this talk with my
father, I received a gift in the mail from a
friend of mine. It was a book of daily affir-
mations with one affirmation listed for
each day of the year.

It has been my experience that when you
get something with days of the year on it,
you automatically turn to the page that lists
your own birthday.

I hurriedly opened the book to November
tenth to see what words of wisdom this
book had in store for me. I did a double take
and tears of disbelief and appreciation rolled
down my face. There, on my birthday, was
the exact same poem that had helped my
father for all these years!

It is called The Serenity Prayer:

> *God, grant me the Serenity to accept the
> things I cannot change; the Courage to
> change the things I can; and the Wisdom
> to know the difference.*

Barry Spilchuk

More Chicken Soup?

Many of the stories and poems you have just read were submitted by readers such as yourself who read other volumes of *Chicken Soup for the Soul*. We publish at least five or six *Chicken Soup for the Soul* books every year. So we invite you, too, to share a story, poem or article that you feel belongs in a future volume of *Chicken Soup for the Soul*.

Stories may be up to 1,200 words and must uplift or inspire. This may be a story you clip out of the local newspaper, a magazine, or a church or company newsletter. It may be something you receive on the fax, a favorite quotation you have on the refrigerator door, a poem you have written or a personal experience that has deeply touched you.

Just send a copy of your favorite stories and other pieces to us at this address.

Chicken Soup For The Soul
P.O. Box 30880
Santa Barbara, CA 93130
fax: 805-563-2945
To e-mail or visit our Web sites:
www.chickensoup.com
www.clubchickensoup.com

We will be sure to credit both you and the author for your submission. Thank you for your contribution.

For information about speaking engagements, other books, audiotapes, workshops and
training programs, please contact any of our
authors directly.

Who Is Jack Canfield?

Jack Canfield is one of America's leading experts in the development of human potential and personal effectiveness. He is both a dynamic, entertaining speaker and a highly sought-after trainer. Jack has a wonderful ability to inform and inspire audiences toward increased levels of self-esteem and peak performance.

He is the author and narrator of several bestselling audio- and videocassette programs, including *Self-Esteem and Peak Performance, How to Build High Self-Esteem, Self-Esteem in the Classroom* and *Chicken Soup for the Soul—Live.* He is regularly seen on television shows such as *Good Morning America, 20/20* and *NBC Nightly News.* Jack has coauthored numerous books, including the *Chicken Soup for the Soul* series, *Dare to Win* and *The Aladdin Factor* (all with Mark Victor Hansen), *100 Ways to Build Self-Concept in the Classroom* (with Harold C. Wells) and *Heart at Work* (with Jacqueline Miller).

Jack is a regularly featured speaker for professional associations, school districts, government agencies, churches, hospitals, sales organizations and corporations. His clients have included the American Dental Association, the American Management Association, AT&T, Campbell Soup, Clairol, Domino's Pizza, GE, ITT, Hartford Insurance, Johnson & Johnson, the Million Dollar Roundtable, NCR, New England Telephone, Re/Max, Scott Paper, TRW and Virgin Records. Jack is also on the faculty of Income Builders International, a school for entrepreneurs.

Jack conducts an annual eight-day Training of Trainers program in the areas of self-esteem and peak performance. It attracts educators, counselors, parenting trainers, corporate trainers, professional speakers, ministers and others interested in developing their speaking and seminar leading skills. For further information about Jack's books, tapes and training programs, or to schedule him for a presentation, please contact:

Self-Esteem Seminars
P.O. Box 30880 • Santa Barbara, CA 93130
Phone: 805-563-2935 • Fax: 805-563-2945
Web site: *www.chickensoup.com*

Who Is Mark Victor Hansen?

Mark Victor Hansen is a professional speaker who, in the last twenty years, has made over four thousand presentations to more than 2 million people in thirty-two countries. His presentations cover sales excellence and strategies; personal empowerment and development; and how to triple your income and double your time off.

Mark has spent a lifetime dedicated to his mission of making a profound and positive difference in people's lives. Throughout his career, he has inspired hundreds of thousands of people to create a more powerful and purposeful future for themselves while stimulating the sale of billions of dollars worth of goods and services.

Mark is a prolific writer and has authored *Future Diary, How to Achieve Total Prosperity* and *The Miracle of Tithing.* He is coauthor of the *Chicken Soup for the Soul* series, *Dare to Win* and *The Aladdin Factor* (all with Jack Canfield) and *The Master Motivator* (with Joe Batten).

Mark has also produced a complete library of personal empowerment audio- and videocassette programs that have enabled his listeners to recognize and use their innate abilities in their business and personal lives. His message has made him a popular television and radio personality, with appearances on ABC, NBC, CBS, HBO, PBS and CNN. He has also appeared on the cover of numerous magazines, including *Success, Entrepreneur* and *Changes.*

Mark is a big man with a heart and spirit to match—an inspiration to all who seek to better themselves.

You can contact Mark at:

MVH & Associates
P.O. Box 7665
Newport Beach, CA 92658
Phone: 714-759-9304 or 800-433-2314
Fax: 714-722-6912
Web site: *www.chickensoup.com*

Who Is Barry Spilchuk?

Barry Spilchuk is a professional speaker and trainer, and has been dubbed Canada's Dale Carnegie.

Barry's purpose is to inspire others to have a greater degree of love in their life. His special niche is teaching corporate executives *How to Fall in Love* through his Executive Esteem Program.

Barry has coauthored *The Magic of Masterminding* and has a very effective tape series that enhances relationships entitled "Talk to Me."

Barry's clients include corporations, sales organizations, school boards, hospitals and not-for-profit groups. For further information on scheduling Barry for a presentation, please contact him at:

P.O. Box 21088
North Bay, Ontario, Canada P1B 9N8
Phone: 888-88BARRY
Fax: 705-497-5941

Contributors

Many of the stories in this book were taken from books we have read. These sources are acknowledged in the Acknowledgments section. Some of the stories and poems were contributed by friends of ours, who, like us, are professional speakers. If you would like to contact them for information on their books, tapes and seminars, you can reach them at the addresses and phone numbers provided below.

Dr. Dan S. Bagley III is a professor of Mass Communications at the University of South Florida in Tampa. Coauthor of the internationally acclaimed book *Beyond Selling,* Dan conducts seminars on communication, influence and creativity. 813-962-2748.

MaryAnn LoSchiavo Barbuto lives with her husband and two sons in Brooklyn, New York, and continues to write. E-mail: *FourMagick@aol.com.*

Paul Barton is the father of two children. He has worked in the financial services industry for close to twenty years. Presently he teaches financial strategies to people who think they don't have any money! He enjoys running, golfing, curling and hockey. 705-497-3420.

Douglas Paul Blankenship is a highly successful building developer, motivational speaker and author of several articles including "Psychographic View of Transit Riders" and "Do We Still Have a Bill of Rights?" He has four college degrees and is listed in *Who's Who in the World* and *Who's Who in Finance.* He is also a doctor, educator, professor and futurist thinker. 2740 E. Washington Ave., Orange, CA 92669.

Michael T. Burcon is a student at Sherman College of Straight Chiropractic in Spartanburg, South Carolina. He has appeared in the "Up and Coming" section of *People* magazine for selling 1 million Weird Beard natural pizzas. He recently developed the board game called The Board, based upon chiropractic board questions. It sells for $39.95. He can be reached at 188 Williams Road, Chesnee, SC 29323 or call 864-578-1797.

Fr. Brian Cavanaugh, T.O.R., began collecting quotations, anecdotes and stories as a form of journal-writing therapy. He has four books published by Paulist Press and his most recent is *Sower's Seeds Aplenty: Fourth Planting.* He is also a storytelling motivational/inspirational lecturer. He can be contacted at Franciscan University, Steubenville, OH 43952.

Maureen Corral is a teacher of deaf and hard of hearing students in the Rochester City School District. She received her Master's in Deaf Education from New York University. She has survived breast cancer twice. She can be reached at 200 North Avenue, Rochester, NY 14626 or call 716-723-0684.

Hedy J. Dalin is a geriatric social worker. She is a graduate of the University of California at Berkeley and received her Master's in Social Work from Columbia University.

Glen DeVuono has served as manager of the North Bay & District Chamber of Commerce for thirty years. He is a very giving, caring and dedicated man who is devoted to his community. He is single and can be reached at 705-472-8480.

Ronald D. Eberhard, an author and humorist from Grove City, Ohio, calls himself a "people planner." He serves as president of Business and Estate Planning Services Unlimited, which specializes in counseling families in business and other professionals. Ron is a popular banquet speaker and motivational seminar leader. He has compiled a book, *As the Family Whirls,* and publishes a newsletter, *Dream Weaving,* which focuses on the opportunities and challenges of life. P.O. Box 458, Grove City, OH 43123-0458, 614-871-0114.

Elder Vaughn J. Featherstone, after serving in the Presiding Bishopric of the Church of Jesus Christ of Latter-Day Saints since April 1972, was called as a member of the First Quorum of the Seventy of the Church on October 1, 1976.

He is presently serving as president of the North America Northeast Area. Elder Featherstone has also served as president of the Philippines/Micronesia Area; president of the Church's Utah South Area; and as general president of the Young Men, the Church's auxiliary for young men ages twelve to eighteen.

N. Gayle Fischer is a graduate of Drake University in Des Moines, Iowa; Phillips Theological Seminary in Enid, Oklahoma; and North American Baptist Seminary in Sioux Falls, South Dakota, where he received a Doctor of Ministry degree. He served churches in Iowa, Kansas and Sioux Falls. Rev. and Mrs. Fischer have five children, twelve grandchildren and one great-granddaughter.

Wayne Furrow is a blacksmith who is married to Diane and has two daughters, Jennifer and Sarah. He can be reached at 904 Premier Rd. #6, North Bay, Ontario, Canada P1A 2H5 or e-mail at *wfurrow@onlink.net.*

Lin Hardick teaches a program she developed called Life is a Verb! in major cities in the United States and Canada. Her son, B. J., a second-year science student at Queen's University, suggested *Chicken Soup for the Soul* as a perfect venue for Lin's "Wrong Number" story. E-mail: *Blissfindr@aol.com.*

Allan Hirsh, M.A., is a psychotherapist, trainer and cartoonist. He is a strong believer in the healing power of laughter and joy. He uses humor with his clients and in his stress management workshops.

Christine James is a kindhearted spirit. She is a professional crafter and floral designer. She is the decoration chairperson for Butte's Christian Women's Club. Her talent is widely recognized, and her outstanding achievements have allowed her to travel to several cities. You can contact Christine at 610 W. Mercury, Butte, MT 59701.

Steve Kendall hasn't written any books, doesn't lecture in any of the fifty states, hasn't won any awards, isn't recognized as a world traveler and hasn't created any seminars or workshops. Steve is, however, the proud brother of Dave

Kendall. If you want to say hello, you can reach Steve at 510-758-1241 or by fax at 510-758-8610.

Nick Lazaris, Psy.D., is a psychologist and professional speaker whose dynamic seminars help home and small business owners achieve breakthrough results and dramatic business and personal success. Nick can be reached at 1149 Summitridge Drive, Diamond Bar, CA 91765 or call 800-976-1332.

Carl Lewis has won nine gold medals and one silver medal in the Olympic Games. He has won a total of ten world championships: eight gold, one silver and one bronze. Carl was born in Birmingham, Alabama, and grew up in New Jersey. He currently lives in Houston and trains with Tom Tellez at the University of Houston. He is a member of the Santa Monica Track Club where he has been a leader in creating an esprit de corps and family-type closeness.

Mike Lynott is vice president of Group R, a New Jersey-based information systems consulting firm. He lives with his wife, Nancy, and children, Rachel and Sean, on the Jersey shore. For as long as he can remember, Mike has been listening to and retelling stories of his Irish-American family from northeastern Pennsylvania.

Hanoch McCarty, Ed.D., is one of the most sought-after motivational speakers whose corporate training programs focus on strategies that build employee and customer loyalty as well as free creativity and maximize personal productivity. His work uses the bottom line power of kindness and integrity. He can be reached at Learning Resources, PO Box 66, Galt, CA 95632 or e-mail *kindness@softcom.net.*

Donna McDermott is an educator, lecturer and Nationally Certified Stress Management Consultant. She is the founder and director of Family Stress Management and the Center for Excellence in Phoenix, Arizona. She specializes in resolving stresses that create illness and block us from manifesting our full potential. *From the Heart of a Joyful Child* is available in a 16x21 full color poster by sending a money order for $12.95 to Family Stress Management, PO Box 37791, Phoenix, AZ

85069. Donna can be reached at 602-433-9414 for consultations and lecture appearances.

Molly Melville grew up in upstate New York. She now lives in Orlando, Florida, along with her sister Maggie. Molly's hobbies are singing, dancing, rollerblading and attending the University of Central Florida. Her favorite thing to do is to vacation in Key West!

Larry Miller has been photographing weddings for over twenty years. He holds two national degrees bestowed by the Professional Photographers of America. In 1995 Larry was inducted into the Tennessee Professional Photographers Hall of Fame. 115 Reese Road, Sevierville, TN 37862, 423-453-5547.

Alice Cravens Moore has taught school for twent-six years. She is a public speaker and the author of three books, *A New Song, Ways Which Be in Christ* and *Comforted of God*. She lives with her family in Humboldt, Tennessee.

Cari Morrison is a freelance consultant, wife, mother and grandmother. She is a Bible and inspirational speaker and is currently pursuing her Master's of Counseling.

Tammy Litchfield Najjar is a native of Cadiz, Kentucky. She was a fire/safety trainer for Opryland Corp., Nashville, Tennessee, from 1983 to 1986 and an office manager for Hitachi America from 1986 to 1991. She is married and has three children. She currently lives in Riverside, California.

Joanie Nietsche, affectionately known as the "Wild Woman," is an inspirational keynote speaker and professional development trainer who is noted for bringing high energy, humor and heart to her presentations. She is the author of *Unleash the Wild Woman!: 101 Ways to Raise Your Self-Esteem and Reclaim Your Personal Power.* Joanie can be reached at Wild Woman Presentations, P.O. Box 800359, Dallas, TX 75380 or by calling 214-342-9991.

Kim Noone is a freshman at Upper Arlington High School in Columbus, Ohio. In her spare time she enjoys track, water polo, photography and traveling. She likes learning and plans to attend college and get a job in elementary education or zoology.

Paula Petrovic is a consultant, facilitator, teacher and author. Through her company SANDWORKS™ she utilizes self-discovery techniques to assist clients in attaining new heights of success. Her joy is empowering people to actualize their dreams. She can reached at P.O. Box 1541, Sedona, AZ 86339.

Laurie Pines quit a high-paying, high-tech job in Silicon Valley to pursue her lifelong dream of teaching. Currently she teaches mathematics in Milpitas, California. A mother of two teenagers, she finds time to play soccer and to act in community theater.

Charlie Plumb was recently selected as one of America's top ten motivational speakers. Charlie inspires audiences to turn adversity into advantage. His autobiography, *I'm No Hero,* is in its twenty-fifth printing. For more information on Mr. Plumb's speaking engagements call 805-683-1969 or e-mail *plumbtalk@aol.com.*

Kelly Ranger lives in North Bay, Ontario, Canada. She works full time as a Customer Service Officer at Canada Trust but her most important and inspiring role is a mother to sons Aaron and Justin, and as a wife to her husband, Richard.

Nancy Richard-Guilford is an author and inspiring speaker who ignites audiences with her passion for life and contagious high energy. Known for her proven practical strategies, her client list ranges from metaphysical churches to the U.S. Navy. Author of the upcoming *Yikes!—Time for Plan B,* she is coarranger on husband James Guilford's "Makin' Happy Music" CD. You can reach Nancy by writing to P.O. Box 24220, Ventura, CA 93002 or call 805-648-6590.

Brenda Rose is an artist and animal communicator living on Maui with her husband, David. She works with wild animals in captivity helping their needs become known and fulfilled. Wild animals and their wisdom are the subject of her art.

John Sandquist is a lifelong resident of Blue Island, Illinois (the City on the Hill). He spent his childhood in a loving household with three wonderful sisters who taught him early on who was always right and what not to ask. Their friendship and that lesson continues.

Shari Smith, a former middle-school math teacher in Texas and Florida, is currently the Income Development Director for the American Cancer Society in Austin, Texas. Her motivation for teaching and helping others is derived from her family, her students and her relationship with Christ.

Dee M. Taylor is a thirty-two-year-old mother of four; two of her daughters were adopted as teenagers. She has no special qualifications. Her inspiration for her contribution and her life is her mother, who is as near an angel as is humanly possible. She lives in Rockville, Indiana.

Marilyn L. Teplitz is president of MLT Resources of Virginia Beach, Virginia, specializing in human resources management consulting and training in the areas of sexual harassment and employee relations. She also conducts sexual harassment investigations for federal agencies and private companies. "Reminder" is dedicated to her parents, George and "Sis" Mattingly, who died within nine months of each other. Marilyn can be reached at 219 53rd Street, Virginia Beach, VA 23451 or by calling 804-437-9101.

Bonnie J. Thomas was an elementary teacher and later a secretary at Iowa State University before retiring to beautiful Lake of the Ozarks. She is a widow, mother of three lovely daughters and grandmother of four. Her hobbies are writing, singing and playing piano.

Kevin Toole is a sixth grade student at Mounds Park Academy in St. Paul, Minnesota. He enjoys skateboarding, Rollerblading, biking, basketball, horseback riding and snowboarding. He loves animals but especially enjoys his cat, hamster and horses. He also enjoys helping the needy and homeless.

Roberta Tremblay lives in Chino, California, with her husband and two sons. "Simply Said" is a true story that happened to Roberta and her friend in 1995. The story was so touching she wanted to share it with others.

Henry Matthew Ward is a Realtor and home builder in Murfreesboro, Tennessee. His hobbies are classical music and writing poetry. He can be reached at 615-890-2178.

Mary Jane West-Delgado is a physical therapist of twenty years and currently teaches Ergonomics/Back Safety on the job. She is an author of short stories and cartoons and corporate president of Comfort Z-Z-Zone, marketing safety products of her own design.

Chrystle White was born in Mississippi and raised in New Orleans. She hails from a "sound mind and Southern Baptist" upbringing. Chrystle is the mother of two and resides in Florida, where her husband is an entertainer.

Jeff Yalden is a nationally recognized motivational speaker and publisher of the newsletter *Motivate*. Jeff has overcome a learning disability and depression, and enjoys sharing the secrets of his success with others. He is a former United States Marine and was elected Mr. New Hampshire Male America. Jeff speaks to high school and junior high students about his "Game Plan for Life." He can be reached at 22A Main Street, Hollis, NH 03049 or by calling 800-948-9289.

Permissions

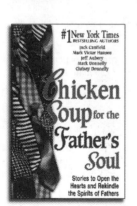

Coming Fall 2001

Code #9373 • Paperback • $12.95

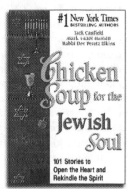

Code #8989 • Paperback • $12.95

Code #9330 • Paperback • $12.95

Code #942X • Paperback • $12.95

Also Available in Quality Paperback

A Cup of Chicken Soup for the Soul
Chicken Soup for the Cat & Dog Lover's Soul
Chicken Soup for the Christian Family Soul
Chicken Soup for the Christian Soul
Chicken Soup for the College Soul
Chicken Soup for the Country Soul
Chicken Soup for the Couple's Soul
Chicken Soup for the Expectant Mother's Soul
Chicken Soup for the Father's Soul
Chicken Soup for the Gardener's Soul
Chicken Soup for the Golden Soul
Chicken Soup for the Golfer's Soul
Chicken Soup for the Kid's Soul
Chicken Soup for the Little Souls
Chicken Soup for the Mother's Soul, Vol. I, II
Chicken Soup for the Parent's Soul
Chicken Soup for the Pet Lover's Soul
Chicken Soup for the Preteen Soul
Chicken Soup for the Single's Soul
Chicken Soup for the Soul, Vol. I–VI
Chicken Soup for the Soul at Work
Chicken Soup for the Soul Cookbook
Chicken Soup for the Sports Fan's Soul
Chicken Soup for the Surviving Soul
Chicken Soup for the Teenage Soul, Vol. I, II, III
Chicken Soup for the Teenage Soul Journal
Chicken Soup for the Teenage Soul Letters
Chicken Soup for the Unsinkable Soul
Chicken Soup for the Woman's Soul, Vol. I, II
Chicken Soup for the Writer's Soul
Condensed Chicken Soup for the Soul
Sopa de Pollo para el Alma, Vol. I, II, III
Sopa de Pollo para el Alma de la Madre
Sopa de Pollo para el Alma de la Mujer
Sopa de Pollo para el Alma del Adolescente
Sopa de Pollo para el Alma del Trabajador
Sopa de Pollo para el Alma del Cristiano